THE NEW WORLD ORDER'S DEFINING CRISES

The New World Order's Defining Crises

The Clash of Promise and Essence

C.G. JACOBSEN
Professor of Political Science and Director
Eurasian Security Studies
Carleton University

Dartmouth

Aldershot • Brookfield USA • Singapore • Sydney

Published by
Dartmouth Publishing Company Limited
Gower House
Croft Road
Aldershot
Hants GU11 3HR
England

Dartmouth Publishing Company
Old Post Road
Brookfield
Vermont 05036
USA

British Library Cataloguing in Publication Data
Jacobsen, Carl G. (Carl Gustav), 1944-
  The new world order's defining crises : the clash of
  promise and essence
  1.Mediation, International 2.International cooperation
  I.Title
  327'.09049

Library of Congress Cataloging-in-Publication Data
Jacobsen, C. G. (Carl G.)
  The new world order's defining crises : the clash of promise and
  essence / C.G. Jacobsen.
      p.   cm.
  Includes bibliographical references and index.
  ISBN 1-85521-883-6 (hb)
  1. World politics–1989- I. Title.
  D860.J32   1996
  909.82–dc20   96-18841
                                                                      CIP

ISBN 1 85521 883 6

Printed and bound in Great Britain by Hartnolls Limited, Bodmin, Cornwall

Contents

Acknowledgments: A special thank you to my family, whose patience, understanding and support made this book possible. My son, Kai Brand-Jacobsen, designed the cover, and also provided invaluable editorial help--as did a number of friends and colleagues. Finally, a thank you to Debbie Williams, the cartographer who prepared the war zone maps that appear at the end of chapters three, four and five.

1 Introduction

The disintegration of the Soviet Union directly and indirectly sparked proclamations of End to Communism, New World Order and even End of History--or at least the History of ideologies and ideological conflict. The theses challenged every area of my expertise, as Soviet/Russian specialist, and as lecturer on international affairs and conflict studies. As such, they led directly to intensified research into the particulars of later chapter themes (beginning with chapter 5), and to course revisions that chartered this book's overall structure, scope and vision.

A first focus, complementing the revisiting of the dynamics that unravelled the Soviet Union, was to reexamine the reality and essential myths of the Old World Order. A second focus originated in the Gulf War, the immediate occasion for US President Bush's declaration of New World Order, then extended to in-depth monitoring of the two other conflict zones of the early transitional years--Yugoslavia and the volatile southern periphery of the former USSR, with its Moldova/Transdniester, Crimean, Abkhazi-Georgian, Nagorno-Karabakh (Armenian/Azeri) and Tajik conflict nodes.

Both the particular sub-themes and the larger totality have benefited from considerable feedback, the former from readers of the earlier chapter and article forms in which they originally appeared (in the Michael Cox edited *Soviet Collapse and the Post-Communist World: A Critical Reassessment*, the *Bulletin for Peace Proposals, European Security* and *War & Society*), the latter from my students.

The choice of conflicts as the weathervanes of the supposed New World Order is partly because it was one of these that actually spawned its proclamation, partly because the others--perhaps more than the first--have effectively defined the parameters of end-of-the-Century international relations, and thus the essence of the prevailing Order, whether Old or New.

There have of course been other conflicts; a recent Pugwash conference counted 44 current conflicts that had cost more than 1000 lives, of which the UN had evinced interest in less than half. And some have been more vicious, certainly that in Rwanda, which saw the massacre of some 500,000 Tutsis in 1994. But no other has seen the 'international community' response of the Gulf War, and no other has seen the immediacy of global

3

strategic interests associated with Yugoslavia and Russia's 'Near Abroad'--not least the facts and ramifications of un-accounted-for nuclear weapons and materiel, and hungry, unemployed nuclear scientists.

The fact of neglect of other conflicts does impact on the question of underlying myths and their relevance: thus, why did the US/UN intervene in Somalia, and not the neighbouring Sudanese civil war, which arguably occasioned more deaths, killings, rape, starvation and other abominations? Was it just because Katherine Hepburn was pictured with a child victim in Mogadishu by CNN cameras? And why did we intervene in Bosnia and not in Tajikistan or Nagorno-Karabakh, or the more truly genocidal East Timoran and Rwandan tragedies? Was it just because of the power of money--a partisan PR campaign that spent more than a million dollars a day? Who or what determines the moral parameters?

The many unattended-to or insufficiently-attended-to issues of the New World Order also perturb.[1] We are unquestionably using some resources, not least water aquifers, at unsustainable rates, and others in such fashion as to dangerously degrade the environment. We are countenancing spreading levels of poverty, deprivation and desperation that are unsustainable in a world of increasingly accessible and ever-cheaper weapons and knowledge of mass destruction. The globalization of economic structures and interchange, with some 80 per cent of cross-border interactions related to currency speculation (now more than a trillion dollars a day) rather than trade or investment, has deprived governments of basic tools of fiscal management, and exposed standards of living and development to grave risk. The spread of ethno-religious fanaticism and exclusive nationalism has dramatically increased the need for conflict avoidance and control mechanisms, peace-keeping and making, just as financial crisis caused by members, especially US dues payment arrears compels the UN to divert funds from these already underfunded accounts to basic housekeeping.[2]

The urgency of non-sustainable rates of population growth, resource depletion and environmental degradation, a dangerously under-regulated global economy, the mushrooming of inter and intra-group conflict, enfeebled if not emasculated collective will and purpose, and a fundamentally skewered Old World informational menu (pitting CNN and smaller rich world satellite networks against the far lesser reach of Internet anarchy and

---

[1] See C.G. Jacobsen, Morris Miller, Metta Spencer and Eric Tollefsen, ed.s--for Pugwash--, *World Security; The New Challenge*, Toronto: Science for Peace/Dundurn, 1994, Chapters 7 (Why Control Population?), 10 (Global Governance to Address the Crises of Debt, Poverty and Environment), 11 (Reducing the Impact of Fossil-Fuel Burning--Steps Toward Environmental Sustainability), 12 (Energy Alternatives for Sustainable Environmental Security) and 13 (Estimated Costs and Benefits).

[2] See ie 'UN faces its worst cash crisis yet', *Guardian Weekly*, 8 October 1995.

alternative and developing world media), all define a New World Order in waiting, a New World Order of global challenges that defy traditional sovereign state solutions. The financing of sustainable development, the health and education breakthroughs needed to end the horrors of developmental deprivation, and peace-keeping and making, is clearly manageable--not least through minimal taxation of just speculative transactions.[3] The political will, however, remained glaringly absent through the first years of the supposed New Order.

In that sense, this book is testimony to the hollowness and inadequacy of early New World Order rhetoric and policy response. In so doing, however, it may also, hopefully, clarify the dichotomy between what is and what must be. If it helps de-mystify reality and spotlight the real choices that must be made, it will have served its purpose.

---

[3] See World Security, *op. cit.*, Chapters 10 and 13; the latter also present estimates from Worldwatch Institute's State of the World reports, World Game Institute and other calculations and analyses.

2　Reflections on Myths and Politics

ABSTRACT: Examples from the US, Europe and Asia make the case that ethnocentric and biased 'histories' resting on self-serving myths and selective manipulation of news and information were defining parameters of the Old World Order. The dominant theses of the New World Order--not least that which proclaimed 'the death of Communism', and its corollary 'the end of History'-- appear as dubious, and as self-serving. Indeed, today's defining parameters remain, essentially, those of the past.

The Old/New World Order

The New World Order threatens to degenerate into something drearily familiar. It now looks quite as prone to self-serving and manipulated myth-preservation and myth-making, tribal ethnocentrism and the politics of fear and exclusion, as were older world orders.[4] If we cannot transcend the distorting bounds of our group or national cultures, then visions of a more just and less conflict-prone order will remain a mirage--the Holy Grail of our illusion, or delusion.

Parochial histories tell the tale--and illustrate the scope of the challenge. Today's predominant power is as susceptible to the foibles of arrogance and conceit as were and are others.

The American myth of invincibility lingers, dangerously, notwithstanding Vietnam, 1814 and other reverses--perhaps more so now that the Vietnam Syndrome has been expunged by the Gulf War, and its Cold War rival is prostrate. The celebrating of real victory can also distort. Glorification of Texas' 'fight for independence', for example, stands in sharp contrast to Latin American views. The latter see the story as the West saw Moscow's 1979 invasion of Afghanistan, with pretexts for war wilfully manipulated, to justify invasion,

---

[4] C.G. Jacobsen, 'On the search for a new world security order: 'the inviolability of borders'; prescription for peace--or war?', *European Security*, Vol 1 No 1, March 1992, pp 50-57.

7

and annexation [though Russia's earlier absorption of Central Asian states would be a truer analogy].[5]

America's 50th commemoration of Japan's 1941 attack on Pearl Harbour provided another classic example. The surprise nature of Japan's attack was 'perfidious'. Yet that was how Japan had attacked before, as against the Russians in 1904; if she was going to strike, there was every reason to expect surprise assault. Commentators also ignored the fact that the United States had established an oil embargo that promised to cripple Japanese industry, and presented an ultimatum and deadline for Japanese withdrawals from China that was physically impossible to meet. The view from Tokyo was and is different.

Ironically, the United States itself launched most of its wars with surprise attack. The list runs from Indian Wars to more recent campaigns: the Bush Administration's 1989 attack on Panama; the Reagan Administration's strikes against Libya, invasion of Grenada, and war-by-proxy against Nicaragua; the Carter Administration's ill-fated hostage rescue mission against Iran; the Nixon Administration's secret wars against Cambodia and Laos; the Johnson Administration's escalation of the Vietnam War to North Vietnam, and invasion of the Dominican Republic.

But if the New World is prone to myth, the Old World is no less so. One typical example is the image of Richard the Third bequeathed to us through Shakespeare: a hunchback, ugly to behold, disliked by his people, a poor ruler, who murdered the princes who were rightful heirs. Yet a review of local and church records of his time shows a different Richard. He had no hunchback; he is described as handsome, well liked, widely admired and respected; and it appears that the princes may all have outlived him--in the dungeons of the Tower of London.[6]

The fault is not Shakespeare's. He merely passes on the history of his times. It was the history of Tudor propagandists, designed to justify and legitimize Henry Vll's seizure of power after Richard's death.

The historiography of victors and successful usurpers of power finds no better example than Joseph Stalin's Short Course History of the CPSU [Communist Party of Soviet Union], which utterly distorted the cataclysmic events of 1917, and after.[7] It rewrote every stage of the Bolshevik Revolution, excised the name of Leon Trotsky--whose role was as crucial as Lenin's--and others, as well as any mention of Lenin's desperate, dying struggle

---

[5] Peter H. Smith, *Mexico, The Quest for a U.S. Policy*, New York: Foreign Policy Association, 1980, pp 6-8.

[6] Josephine Tey, *The Daughter of Time*, New York and Toronto: Penguin, 1989, pp 172-188.

[7] *Istoriia Vsesoiuznoi Kommunisticheskoi Partii (Bolshevikov)*, Moscow: Gospolizdat, 1938.

against Stalinist dictatorship and chauvinism.[8] Stalin, a peripheral 'grey blur' in the true history of 1917 (in the word's of its foremost historian[9]), is here presented as its most influential figure.

When this author first visited China, in 1971, the history museum was closed; a notice on the door explained that history was being reexamined--the disarming honesty of the announcement was novel; the underlying reality was not.

The self-servingly selective nature of national histories is evident in the myopia that bedevil Russo-Japanese relations. When Russia looks at Japan, she remembers Japan's surprise attack on Port Arthur in 1904, the fact that Japan's interventionary troops were the last to leave after the Revolution, the expansionary forays of Japan's armies in the late 1930s (finally defeated at Lake Khazan and Khalkin Gol), Japan's forward role in America's postwar security system, and Tokyo's later refusal to accept the southern Kurile boundary line that had been sanctioned by both the US and its own government of the time.

Japan remembers only early Russian challenges to its own designs for mainland expansion, Moscow's devastating attack on her Manchurian bastion in the waning days of World War 2 (ignoring the fact that this attack was sought and approved by Washington), the ending of Japanese rights in the southern Kuriles, and the threat of Soviet nuclear arms.[10]

It is the same proclivity that allows Israelis and Palestinians, like Croats and Serbs, to remember only the other's evils--which are then seen to justify and legitimize those that they perpetrate.[11]

Another aspect of the different universes fixture of national histories is illustrated by the fact that French generals, seen in French texts as crucial to Washington's victory in the American Revolution (which of course was, rather, the first Civil War), are absent or only incidental to US histories; Benedict Arnold, hero of British and Canadian texts, is **the** quintessential traitor in US accounts.

The point is not just that 'my terrorist is your freedom fighter; my freedom fighter is your terrorist', though history's judgement on these matters can be capricious. Vidkun Quisling, Norway's Nazi collaborator, whose last name became a synonym for traitor, would

---

[8] Moshe Lewin, *Lenin's Last Struggle*, New York: Monthly Review Press, 1978.

[9] N.N. Sukhanov, *The Russian Revolution 1917*, Oxford: OUP, 1955, pg 2301.

[10] C.G. Jacobsen, *Strategic Power: USA/USSR*, London & New York: Macmillan & St. Martin's Press, 1990, pp 346-351.

[11] Edward W. Said, *The Question of Palestine*, New York: Times Books, 1980; R.A. Reiss, *Report Upon the Atrocities Committed by the Austro-Hungarian Army During the First Invasion of Serbia*, London: Simkin, 1915.

9

clearly have emerged differently from the historiography of Nazi victory. Menachim Begin's terrorist past, including the 1946 carnage at the King David Hotel, appalled Israel's founders (David Ben Gurion demanded that he be deprived of his citizenship); yet a different context later allowed him to emerge as statesman, and Prime Minister. And there were and are many others.

*

The arrogant, racist-tinged myths that justified and drove colonial exploitation and expansion continue to reverberate in British, French, German and other societies. They are echoed in America's creed of **manifest destiny**, in Israel's **chosen people**, in Russia's self-image as guarantor of faith and fount of civilization (under Tsars and Commissars alike), in China's Middle Kingdom alter ego (again, no less so today than under older dynasties), and in Japan's notions of racial purity, and superiority. Interestingly, the more absolutist (and hence racist) of these self-images all derive from scriptures, whose Churches and interpreters have historically, through policies of Crusades and exclusion, legitimized, exacerbated and rivalled the destructiveness of virulent nationalism.

The ideologies with which we sometimes cloak our prejudices, our instincts and fears, are equally deceptive. The self-proclaimed communism of Stalin's and post-Stalin's USSR was in many ways the ultimate perversion, indeed antithesis, of that espoused by Karl Marx, and proved only that dictatorship can as easily adopt communist as it can capitalist garb. Stalin's Marxism was shallow, if not nonexistent. If anything, his *modus operandi*, governing style and system, was that of Ivan the Terrible--whose Russian nickname is more properly and more evocatively translated as Ivan the Awesome.

The same holds true of, for example, Mao Zedong. He also cannot be shown to have read the works of Marx, though he may have read some of Trotsky's. Still, if 5 per cent of his ideology can be ascribed to Marxist influences, there is little doubt that 95 per cent was rooted in Chinese culture, in the aspirations and dreams of the Taiping and other rebellions of the 19th century.

But if the communism of our lazy theologies was false, then so was the capitalism. A Republican US President, Richard Nixon, introduced the first modicum of Medicare, though some of his countrymen had derided it as a communist evil. Other administrations introduced female and universal suffrage, principles of elected and recallable officials and limited unemployment insurance schemes--other ideas initially dismissed as belonging to Marxism's subversive and nefarious realm.[12] Even when capitalism was at its purest, in the

---

[12] See eg *The [London] Times'* and *The New York Times'* coverage of the Paris Commune of 1870!

days of John D. Rockefeller, his acquisition of Texas' oil fields owed as much and perhaps more to the quality of his hired guns as it did to that of his accountants.[13]

And the Reaganomics creed that closed out the era of superpower duopoly was as much a perversion of its professed ideals as was Moscow's; with a tax system that favoured immediate wealth extraction (over wealth creation) and penalized both savings and longer-term investment, it licensed the feudal obscenity of dying-industry managers awarding themselves salaries more than a hundred times that of their employees, and million dollar bonuses that ultimately struck near-lethal blows at morale and competitiveness. It institutionalized greed **and** obsolescence; it was a caricature, and a perversion of capitalism (though some Marxists, of course, would see the perversion as its truest essence).[14]

*

The 1991 proclamation of a New World Order rested on the theses that Communism had died (and thus also the Cold War), that Soviet successor states had made final choices favouring democracy and capitalism, and that the Gulf War and UN intervention in the post-Yugoslav carnage signalled transition from peace-keeping to peace-making, and a new era of cooperative rather than confrontational crisis containment and resolution. On closer scrutiny, however, these theses appear seriously flawed. Each derived from selective and politicized views of history; each bred precisely the type of partial, self-serving myths that defined older world orders. They were **of** those older orders. Rather than heralding the new, they [again] highlighted the distance that must yet be travelled.

The USSR's Rise and Fall--Marxian aberration or Russian continuum?; policy-makers' myth quotient

The collapse of the Soviet Union in 1991 spawned two dominant theses, that the collapse was inevitable and that it signified the end of Communism. Both deserve challenge. By August 1991 then President Mikhail Gorbachev had ended the Communist Party's right to govern, introduced free, multi-Party elections, secured 70 per cent Referendum approval for a more decentralized Union, and, with Republican leaders, negotiated a confederal

---

[13] Paul A. Baran and Paul M. Sweezy, *Monopoly Capitalism*, New York: Monthly Review Press, 1966.

[14] By 1992 US auto-executives' incomes (topped by Chrysler's Iaccocca, at $4.2 million) averaged five times that of their [more successful] Japanese counterparts, while US auto-workers received less than Japanese.

constitution to that end, to which all but the three Baltic leaders gave their support. Pragmatic evolution was clearly possible, and, in hindsight, probably preferable.

What most observers did not anticipate was that Boris Yeltsin, issuing edicts in finest Tsarist/Commissar tradition even as Gorbachev was addressing Russia's Parliament after his return from Crimean detention (by the failed Putschists), would in effect launch his own coup--Boris the 'Democrat' would usurp legal authority again, in October 1993, giving him a unique niche in Russian history. Nor did many anticipate that Gorbachev, who still commanded sufficient military and paramilitary loyalty to allow other options, which others would surely have chosen, would acquiesce--though he had made the same choice in Eastern Europe, also against the advice and entreaties of some, when faced only with the stark alternatives of force or abdication.[15] In fact, what followed was not foreseeable, for it was neither 'necessary' nor inevitable.

As suggested, what failed in 1991 was neither Communism nor totalitarianism, for the regime was of neither hue (see below). Certainly, some of its representatives continued to espouse ideals of the former, much as later regimes in France continued and continue to embrace ideals of the French Revolution long after Thermidor devoured its over-zealous vanguard. But this was testimony to the resonance of those ideas in the enduring cultures of their histories and lands, and by no means indicative of revolutionary intent or purpose.

I argued long before the demise of the Soviet Union (again, see below), as did others, that the onset of Stalinism eviscerated the Revolution of any true Communist content.[16] Some date its demise earlier. Certainly, Lenin's policies, domestic and external, can be seen as ideology-driven. To argue similarly for his successors' is more problematic.

Early Leninist/Trotskyite policy was internationalist and revolutionary; even where they disagreed over tactics, as with the Brest-Litovsk negotiations to extricate Russia from World War 1, both saw the international cause as transcendent over 'national' interests. Neither felt nationalist qualms about giving up territory and wealth if it would gain time and resources for the larger task of aiding Revolution in Germany and elsewhere, and their purpose very nearly succeeded. Fittingly, Lenin's final and total break with Stalin--too late to be effective--was occasioned precisely by the latter's chauvinism, and **self**-serving dictatorial tendencies.[17] To Lenin, power served other purpose; to Stalin there was no other purpose.

---

[15] See also Chapter 5.

[16] See eg C.G. Jacobsen, in Alva Myrdal and others, *Dynamics of European Nuclear Disarmament*, Nottingham: Spokesman, 1981, pp 31-56.

[17] Moshe Lewin, *Lenin's Last Struggle*, New York: Monthly Review Press, 1978.

The change had been heralded earlier. In foreign policy, the revolutionary era ended when the revolutionary crest waned in West and Central Europe, and Marshal Tukhachevsky was forced to retreat from Warsaw--after Stalin, Political Commissar for one flank, failed to effect the ordered link-up (his subsequent reprimand would later reverberate in the killings of both Tukhachevsky and Trotsky).

The 1922 Rapallo Treaty with Germany signalled Moscow's prioritizing of **state** interests. Thereafter, no Soviet foreign policy initiative would again be unambiguously, solely or even predominantly ideological in either purpose or rationale. Western and Soviet leaders alike habitually found it in their interests to proclaim otherwise. But after 25 years of challenges to Soviet foreign policy classes and audiences in North America and Europe to identify one initiative clearly contrary to national or state purpose, this author can conclude only that there is no convincing case.

This echoes another study by this author (also **before** the fall of whatever fell), of Soviet foreign policy towards the Gulf War, its precipitation, its conduct and its aftermath;[18] see the following chapter. The unambiguous conclusion was that Gorbachev's superficially startling policy innovations, his embrace of collective security and carefully calibrated cooperation with the intrusion of [another] Great Power, in fact fell well within the parameters of established and long-term Russian and Soviet policy towards the Middle East. What startled was the clear continuity of Russian and Soviet policy, from before the Crimean War to today. Gorbachev's posture reflected Moscow's traditional response to temporal weakness. It was sophisticated, but not novel.

Throughout the Soviet era conservative Western politicians, such as former US President Ronald Reagan, his UN Ambassador Jean Kirkpatrick, former British Prime Minister Margaret Thatcher and Senator Jesse Helms during the final years, supported by pundits and [some] dissidents routinely and indiscriminately denounced 'Communist aggression', 'Communist threat', Soviet 'totalitarianism' and 'expansionism'. There were also those on the left who spoke of Soviet abuse and 'imperialism'--but they did not confuse such with 'communism'. Yet the most respected Western historians agree that in his conduct of foreign policy Stalin was 'the supreme realist--patient, shrewd and implacable, the Richelieu of his period'.[19]

---

[18] See Chapter 3; C.G. Jacobsen, 'The Gulf War: Washington's War; Moscow's War', *Bulletin of Peace Proposals* (later renamed *Security Dialogue*), September 1991; 'Moscow and the Gulf War: Old Wine in a New Bottle or New Wine in an Old Bottle', *Securite & Strategies Asie*, Centre de Recherches sur L'Asie, April 1991.

[19] Henry Kissinger, *Diplomacy*, New York: Simon & Schuster, 1994, p 333; see also Adam Ulam, *Expansion and Coexistence: Soviet Foreign Policy 1917-73*, Fort Worth: Holt, Rinehart & Winston, Inc., 1974, p 223; and Nicholas Riasanovsky, *A History of Russia*, Oxford: Oxford University Press, 1993, p 513.

Even after attaining superpower status Moscow in fact intervened abroad, either with direct military force or 'gunboat' diplomacy, less frequently than did her Western rivals.[20] When she first intervened in sub-Saharan Africa, in Angola in 1975 and Ethiopia in 1978, it was in locales where the circumstances restrained the United States from overt response (in Angola she supported an internationally recognized government against opposition aided by troops from South Africa's apartheid regime; in Ethiopia she defended against Somali incursion intent on border revision). And Moscow's advances were no more immutable than those of the West: notwithstanding the Afghan venture, Moscow's international alliance and allegiance network at the end of Leonid Brezhnev's tenure as Party leader was less extensive than when he first took office.[21]

No Soviet leader was as adventurous in distant shores as, for example, the early post-Crimean leadership, which briefly established bases in Tsushima and Villefranca, and sent Naval vessels to Northern US ports during the US Civil War, when it appeared that Britain would recognize the South. Zbigniew Brzezinski's conclusion after comparing the colonialist and neo-colonialist thrust of earlier-industrializing Western states with Soviet Russia's at a similar developmental stage, that the need to pay homage to Marxian tenets may ironically have impeded rather than fuelled Moscow's pursuit of similar ambitions, provides nice counterpoint to the less historically minded.

The need to impute ideological adversity, which clearly transcends its actuality, may be generic. Western postures pre-World War 2 and Cold War were haunting echoes of the ideologizing demonology that characterized British and French coverage of Tsarist Russia in the run-up to the Crimean War (which gave us the term 'jingoism'). And they in turn are equally hauntingly echoed in the aspirations of those, like Senator Helms, who in 1994 advocated larger-scale US intervention on behalf of Bosnian Muslims with the **primary**, explicit goal of drawing sufficient Russian counter-support to Serb fighters to justify a redrawing of the ideological divide.

The causal and more important ideological divide may in fact lie elsewhere, and it is one in which neither side cares much for Moscow's political colouration, real or claimed, except to the extent that it might be manipulated to favour their other agendas. One side was evident in the 'experts panel' convened by US Public Television's MacNeil-Lehrer to analyse the October 1993 showdown in Moscow between President Yeltsin and Parliament. Of four panellists three were economists without area background or expertise; only the

---

[20] See Barry Blechman, *Force Without War*, Washington DC: Brookings, 1978; compare Michael Kidron and Dan Smith, *The War Atlas*, London: Pan Books, 1983.

[21] C.G. Jacobsen, 'Mapping Soviet Influence' (charting and contrasting Moscow's relationships with the nations of the world, 1964 and 1982), *The Miami Herald & Hearst-Ridder* syndication, 14 November 1982.

14

fourth, Jerry Hough, was an area specialist. Hough's insistence that Yeltsin had acted unconstitutionally and that Parliament's impeachment was proper, was dismissed by the others' chorus of praise for Yeltsin the Democrat.

Therein the real divide, between those who, like the MacNeil-Lehrer economists, see US/Western interests as best served through pursuit of perceived trade, investment and influence opportunities in Russia (as Armand Hammer and others saw them in the Soviet Union), and those who, like Helms, see greater gains elsewhere through adversarial relations with Eurasia's giant.[22]

*

'Communism' or Bureautocracy? A more focused look at what actually failed in Moscow appears appropriate. As previously suggested, the equation of Soviet and Communist is facile. It also prevents the drawing of appropriate lessons. What failed was not Karl Marx' communism.[23] This decrees the withering away of the state. It sees the state's only purpose as to protect privilege; without privilege it has no purpose. What failed, of course, was the very opposite: a leviathan of a state, protecting a leviathan of privilege.

What failed also was not Lenin's communism. Lenin founded the Party, and decreed its operating maxim of democratic centralism, a maxim which after his death lost all pretence

---

[22] The arguments of the former are aptly represented in 'Sale of the Century', *The Economist*, 14 May 1994, pp 67-8; see also eg 'After the Fall', *The Economist*, 24 September 1994, pp 77-8, and 'The Eighth Sister', *The Economist*, 15 October 1994, p 93. Conversely, the agenda requiring confrontational dogma rests on a rich Cold War legacy of deliberately exaggerated Soviet threat spectres; see eg C.G. Jacobsen, ed., *Strategic Power: USA/USSR*, London & New York: Macmillan & St. Martin's Press, 1990, Ch.s 4, 7 and 8.

[23] The main problem in discussing 'communism' derives from the ignorance of many of its critics of all but its most peripheral texts--such as *Communist Manifesto*; the problem is compounded by the fact that its adherents are also often ignorant of much of the literature. In part this may be explained by the very richness and diversity of the literature, which, like that on 'democracy', transcends easy summary and simple definition. It may be explained by Marx' focus on German capitalism of the mid-19th century, which makes some of his writings appear outdated; by Rosa Luxemburg's multi-lingual skills and correspondence--the bane of biographers and analysts; by Lenin's extraordinarily prolific, varied and multi-faceted *oeuvre*, which in differing doses can sustain distinctly different legacies; and by the theologies of politicization, which have sometimes obscured the contributions of Trotsky, Gramsci and others. The major stumbling block, however, is the legacy of Stalin and the Cold War: in their embrace of dogma, neither Washington nor Moscow was interested in the nuance of theory or context; both preferred the simplicity of their respective catechisms of 'quotations' and 'selections'--and while those of different Soviet leaders were revised so as to reflect particular agendas, they remained partial, and superficial.

to democracy. And he was not squeamish in launching Red Terror against White--against counter-revolutionaries he was as implacable as Sherman torching Georgia. But democratic centralism to him was not a recipe for the future; it was a means to thwart the Tsar's secret police, and to survive the bleak odds of civil war and foreign interventions.[24] He governed not as leader of the Party, but as Chairman of the Council of People's Commissars (or Ministers). The fateful 1922 decision to give Stalin the post of Party Secretary General, to vet the flow of opportunists and new recruits, was made because more prominent Party members considered it marginal; they chose more 'important' positions.[25]

Lenin did not demand conformity. Lev Kamenev and Grigory Zinoviev, who leaked October plans to force postponement of a coup they thought would fail--the ultimate betrayal--, were welcomed into his cabinet. He encouraged vigorous internal debates, and placed no fetters on the flood of experimentation in literature and arts that marked the early years.[26] When a leadership majority opposed his advocacy of peace with Germany, he accepted the decision. When German troops continued to advance he later secured a one-vote majority for reversal, and acceptance of the peace of Brest-Litovsk--but the threats with which he cajoled were of resignation, **not** retribution. With the waning of civil war and withdrawal of most (though not all) of the foreign armies that sustained it, he ended the stifling grip of War Communism and introduced NEP, the New Economic Policy that

---

[24] See Lenin's correspondence with Rosa Luxembourg, who warned that the Party's organizational structure invited misuse. Note: at its apex democratic centralism is little different from the caucus discipline imposed in British-style Parliamentary systems. Where it differs--and what ultimately allowed the Stalinist perversion--is in its extension of that discipline to **all** Party members, and, perhaps even more crucially, in the corrupting essence of its pre-Gorbachevian insistence on monopoly power. [Lenin, of course, *agreed with* Luxembourg's concern: he saw his Party structure as *pro tem*, dictated by the threat of autocracy and secret police, later by Civil War and interventions; it was not to be a model for the future, either domestically or externally...*sic*]

[25] See ie N.N. Sukhanov's 'The Russian Revolution', and Moshe Lewin's 'Lenin's Last Struggle', *op cit.*

[26] A Soviet joke had novelist Maxim Gorky turn to his companion, Lenin's urbane Commissar of Education Anatoli Lunacharsky, as they passed an *avant garde* exhibit: 'I do not understand this modern art'; Lunacharsky concurred. Punch line: this was the last Soviet Commissar of Education who did not understand art..!

16

brought back the market and small-scale private enterprise.[27] He outlawed formal factions, but still insisted on the free flow of inner-Party debate.

Only when impaired by stroke, looked after by Stalin-appointed doctors who limited his movements and intercepted his mail, did he realize that Stalin, by manipulating elections and rival egos, was turning the Party into an instrument of his personal will. Lenin spent his last year smuggling appeals to Trotsky and others (*viz.* his Last Testament), to act while there was still time, to thwart Stalinist dictatorship.[28] They dallied, and lost. Within little more than a decade, all members of Lenin's inner circle were dead, in exile, or in the *gulag*.

Stalin represented counter-revolution. As noted, Lenin's Party was internationalist, in vision and membership, reflecting the tenets of Marxism, and Lenin's disdain for chauvinism. Stalin's slogan, Socialism In One Country, spoke to a now different Party: Russian, Russified, and chauvinist. His *modus operandi* echoed that of Ivan the Terrible. When **his** successor Party threatened to outvote him, in 1934, he launched the purges that preemptively destroyed those who might still claim independent legitimacy. He crushed, then used the now subservient Church. The secret police became his personal watchdog and enforcer. Law was bent to his will, and his alone. The Red Army's leadership was isolated, then liquidated; tsarist traditions, from epaulettes to ballroom dancing and Kutuzov and Suvorov medals, were reintroduced (only duelling remained illegal!). Stalin anointed himself Commander-in-Chief, and Generalissimo. Culture that did not glorify the regime became punishable by exile, prison or worse.

His successors abandoned the harsher aspects of Stalin's rule. Nikita Khrushchev opened the camps, and appealed for Soviet democracy, 'Return to Socialist Legality' and 'Leninist Norms'. But his harshest denunciation of Stalin, his 'crimes' and 'megalomania' (in his Secret Speech to the 20th Party Congress, in February 1956) remained unpublished. His populism was reigned in. 'Collective leadership' was asserted. The Party sought a new social compact, and to exorcize the demon of dictatorship. But though it had itself suffered perhaps more than any other societal group, or perhaps because of that very terror, it was now determined to protect the privilege of inherited power.

Freed from terror, the **apparat** found that it now controlled the levers of power. The Party had itself become the New Class, the class of the establishment. As such, it was a

---

[27] The question of a 'socialist market' constitutes the single most divisive issue of Marxism today. Opponents see it as an illusion, no more than temporary veneer for the inequities and law-of-the-jungle essence of the 'capitalist' market. Adherents draw more positive lessons from elements of Scandinavian and Japanese market management; they fear that more regulated exchange mechanisms will inevitable degenerate into **bureautocracy** (see text, below).

[28] M. Lewin, Lenin's Last Struggle, *op cit.*

conservative class, concerned above all with the retention of power and perpetuation of privilege, for its sons and daughters, and their sons and daughters. Party officials became the new **boyars**, the noblemen of the day.[29]

The parallel between post-Stalinist, neo-Stalinist rule and that of the later Tsars is quite extraordinary: autocracy--though striving for a benevolent facade; deadeningly extensive and intrusive bureaucracy; concentration of wealth and power; limited scope for private enterprise and initiative (at least prior to 1906); ubiquitous secret police; and exile, or worse, for dissidents.

What failed was not Communism, and no Communist claimed that it was. Soviet officials proclaimed it the goal to which they aspired. Some did so genuinely, others not. Like General Pinochet of Chile, and other 'democratic' dictators, they nurtured and gained nurture from foreign and domestic threats that justified pause on the road to progress. Stalin called himself a communist because of the socialization process of the Revolution, much as Pinochet called himself a democrat, to accord with Chile's cultural tradition, but Stalinism had as little to do with Marx as Pinochet's bloody rule had to do with Plato. As a leading British socialist put it: to blame Marx for Stalin is like blaming Jesus Christ for the Spanish Inquisition. One may imagine the comments of those who observed the collapse of that obscenity: thank God: the death of Christianity!

What failed was also not totalitarianism, which is not to say that some of its masters did not wish it to be. Clearly some aspired to totalitarian power, enforced by overlapping levers of societal control, omnipresent police, informers, and neighbourhood committees--as in Pinochet's Chile. But one problem with the concept is precisely this: the Cold War claim that it applied only to Moscow's dominions was so simplistic and ignorant, and so politicized its meaning, that it also distorted it. The second problem, long evident in the anti-Communism of Cold War emigres, and now dramatized by the voters of both Eastern Europe and former Soviet lands, is that totalitarian aspirations to mold minds or thought failed miserably.

[As in its application also to Nazi Germany, the term totalitarianism has of course become synonymous with ultimate opprobrium. Yet the extreme politicization of its application--as in applying to Cambodia's Khmer Rouge only when **not** allies of Western

---

[29] One joke had Brezhnev bring his mother to Moscow, where he shows off the opulence of his estates and luxury cars; but she leaves, for she fears the vengeance of the bolsheviki. Then there was the serum, to bring back the dead. Lenin is awakened, and offered power, gold and glory, but wants only a room with a desk, and back issues of Pravda. Later...tension builds when he does not emerge, yet who dares disturb him? ...finally, a hesitant, 'collective' knock, and later entry--but there is only a note: 'returned to Switzerland; I must start anew!'. In 1991 Lenin would have stood with the miners (with Trotsky--and Mao's spirit).

will and purpose--has, unfortunately, twisted it into a barometer only of prejudice, and political convenience.]

Soviet specialists in the 1960s used to joke that there were more communists at the University of the Sorbonne in Paris than in the Soviet Union. If it was true then, and it was, it is clearly even more so today. The point is, of course: wishing does not make it so. A totalitarian state cannot exist merely in the dreams of its masters, or the fears of its enemies. Although neo-Stalinist control was at times harshly authoritarian; it was not totalitarian.

But if it was not communist and not totalitarian--except, perhaps, in aspiration--then what was it? The most useful term, because it embodies the essence of all-embracing bureaucracy and autocracy, and also because it facilitates the drawing of appropriate lessons, is **bureautocracy**. Bureaucracy, serving autocracy (Tsar/Politburo), legitimized by faith (Church/Communism), and bound by duty. The formula worked as well for Stalin as it had for the Tsars.

But by the late 1970s the context had changed; the Party's ideological Godfather, Michail Suslov, acknowledged that old formulas no longer worked. The superstructure was no longer appropriate. The base had changed. The country was no longer rural and illiterate; it was urban, educated, and no longer satisfied with the dogmas and homilies of the past. A middle class had emerged, with middle class aspirations and demands. Marx' conditions for Capitalism in Russia--the necessary precursor to Communism--were in fact being met. At the same time, the bureaucracy, able in the past to cope with evolutionary change, and hide or circumvent failure, proved utterly unable to cope with the ever-escalating pace and diversity of the high tech revolution of the late 20th century. It imploded, in escapist corruption and self-serving greed.

Lenin's revolution, with its communist ideal, failed not in 1989, but in 1924, or even earlier. Premature by definition, and so acknowledged by both Lenin and Trotsky (who saw revolution in Germany as its only sustaining hope), its failure followed the pattern of other revolutions that have sought fundamental socioeconomic change. The revolutionary dilemma: the desperation that fuels revolt is profoundly polarizing, compelling embrace of visions that are necessarily utopian--for they must sustain through the darkest hours--, and expectations that no successor government can realize.

Revolutionary government cannot survive without compromise to its ideals. But if this course is precluded or aborted, the disillusioned will join reaction: counter-revolution, in fact if not in name. Real socioeconomic change must rest on cultural change, and as Michail Gorbachev so painfully learned, such change is always excruciatingly slow. The ideals of the French revolution are still not fully achieved. Those of the Paris Commune, such as women's equality and the right to recall elected officials, dubbed communist and subversive by the press barons of the West, are still being fought for. So also with the grander ideals of the Bolsheviki; they will be fought for and quite possibly highjacked and perverted again, whether violently or not, because they also are integral to the yearnings of much of humankind. In Moscow, the perversions of the **system** are repudiated, yet the dreamers' ideals will continue to resonate--and invite manipulation.

The Soviet **apparat** cloaked itself in the rhetoric of Communism. But the rhetoric was Newspeak. To talk of the death of Communism is to adopt that Newspeak. Worse: to assert the death of Communism, with its concepts of equal opportunity and communal responsibility, is to encourage the very kind of rapacious (and narcissistic) capitalism that nurtured early communist dreams, and that will inevitably revive them.

Soviet failure is not the failure of Communism. Rather, relative success and social peace in the West may ironically be due to the fact that capitalist societies were (and could be) forced to adopt more of Communism's demands for equal rights than was Moscow. Moscow failed because its ideals were betrayed, **not** because they were upheld.[30]

There are, as suggested, more appropriate terms for what failed, from neo-Stalinism to state monopoly capitalism[31] and partocracy (if one ignores Gorbachev's reforms). The problem with these is that they also suggest lessons that appear irrelevant to Western societies. The advantage of the term **bureautocracy** lies precisely in the fact that it may be seen to have wider applicability. Autocracy as such may have been expunged from Western culture. Yet a stultifying, self-aggrandizing variant (power sclerosis?) is integral to the increasing bureaucratization of Western administrative structures. In the West also, it alienates regions from centre, people from government. Bureaucracies are governments' arteries; **bureautocracy** hardens and may clog them.

Communism, with its aspiration to truer democracy, is as susceptible to perversion as other visions. But it will remain with us because it also embodies some of our highest ideals--as suggested by those who see Jesus as the quintessential Communist, and Communism as the *sine qua non* of **his** Christianity.[32] Others define 'Communism with a

---

[30] These, of course, concerned the social agenda and the ability to stimulate growth--the essence of the Party's claim to legitimacy--; not democracy as such. Failures of democracy alone do not spark systemic failure. One might note the $20 million plus cost of US Senatorial campaigns, which arguably limits access as effectively as did Party membership in the USSR; escalating costs and single-member constituencies in (other) Parliamentary systems may also allow special interests to thwart the will of the majority.

[31] This, a **consequence** of bureautocracy, and perhaps the greatest single cause of failure, was also the ultimate irony: the market perversions and inevitable inequities of monopoly control epitomized *capitalist* evil(!); see eg Paul A. Baran and Paul M. Sweezy, *Monopoly Capital*, Penguin Books, 1968.

[32] It is not the faith the Marxists decried; it was the fact of an often corrupt Church allied to government, manipulating faith to diffuse opposition, and perpetuate [its] privilege.

human face' as Social Democracy; Alec Nove saw Socialism as 'Capitalism with a human face'. The ideals of our heart may not be as different as we think.

*

Moscow; Back to the Future? The 1991 'Revolution' in Moscow, the implosion of the *ancien regime* and phoenix-like proliferation of new, 'democratic' states, appeared to confirm the New World Order launched and proclaimed by the Gulf War Coalition. Yet the new watchword mirrored politics, not history. History is not kind to too-rapid change. Revolutions devour their children.

The revolutionaries of 1917 sought to destroy an order they saw as unjust, exploitative and corrupt, as did those of 1991. Both sought profound socioeconomic change, universal rights and opportunities. The **Bolsheviki** were buoyed by the revolutionary wave that appeared to sweep Europe after World War 1. In 1991 expectations of bountiful aid sustained visions of rapid transformation. But Europe's post World War 1 revolutionary wave ran out; the nation turned back to chauvinism and autocracy. The hopes and illusions of 1991 fades as fast. By Summer 1992 sustaining visions were already frayed; opinion polls traced the rise of law and order, and nationalist orthodoxies.[33]

A different analogy, between the last Tsarist years and the interim governments of 1917 on the one hand and today's democrats on the other, is also intriguing. The lure of Istanbul and the Bosporus, promised by London and Paris at the outbreak of World War 1, brought Tsarist offensives when Germany threatened breakthroughs in the West; they relieved the Allies, but doomed the Tsar. The successor Provisional governments acknowledged the need for peace, land redistribution and fair elections. Yet again, and instead, the Straits promise brought another offensive at Allied urging, an offensive that relieved them, but shredded regime support at home. In 1991 and later the lure was Western aid and investment, in return for adopting Western economic prescriptions. Yet, as actual aid lagged ever-further behind promises (sometimes addressing donors' needs more than Russia's), an increasing number of reformers embraced regime opponents' refrain that this price also was a mirage, and that the cost of adhering to an 'alien' prescription was likely to worsen rather than improve the economic crisis.[34]

---

[33] According to a September 1992 opinion poll, 80% felt they lived better before Gorbachev unleashed the first reforms, 67% favoured [past] socialism, and 50% had a positive view of Stalin (up from 29% in a September 1991 poll); from *Moskovskaya Pravda*, reprinted in The *Ottawa Citizen*, 26 September 1992.

[34] See ie 'Rutskoi finds favour as Yeltsin's star fades', the [London] *Sunday Times*, 23 August 1992.

21

There are sharper analogies, as well as some major differences, between then and now. After 1917 Russia lost one-third of its population and one-fourth of its territory, including most of its iron and steel industries, the food-producing region of the Ukraine, Belorussia, Finland and the Baltic territories. Independence proclamations by Caucasian and Central Asian and other territories followed. Most were reabsorbed by 1926, but it was not until World War 2 that older Russian boundaries were reestablished--minus Poland and Finland. The rush to secession and independence in late 1991 reflected similar centrifugal dynamics, again fed by the confluence of socioeconomic crisis, the collapse of old and uncertainty of new central power. By 1994 Russia was asserting a security sphere or interest throughout the 'Near Abroad', with particular responsibility for the Russian diaspora.[35]

In 1918, beset by rapidly spreading civil war, foreign interventions in support of White armies, and a collapsing economy, the Bolsheviks introduced War Communism, and harsh grain and other requisition policies. In 1992-93 also, the ideals of theory were soon buffeted by reality and circumstance. Boris Yeltsin, as Gorbachev, failed to privatize most agricultural production, yet had little choice; the first peasant survey showed only one percent ready to accept the uncertain promise and insecurity of private ownership. By 1992 some peasant collectives began to withhold produce and cut output in response to harvest price increases falling behind those of industrial goods--as had farmers in the late 1920s. Governments in Kiev and elsewhere again felt forced to impose and sometimes enforce state-priced requisition demands.[36]

Another analogy affects personnel. In 1918 Party ranks were swelled by opportunists and careerists. In 1991, some 'democratic' leaders were erstwhile supporters of the hardliners' coup--who embraced the new faith only after the coup's failure. In 1991 as in 1917 revolutionaries proclaimed socioeconomic transformation, but the bureaucrats, administrators and managers needed to effect the new order were *perforce* trained by the old. In 1918 'old specialists' flooded into the Red Army, new Ministries and organizations. In 1992-'94 also, notwithstanding new names and the exclusion of those most prominently tainted by the old, the corridors of power and influence continued to be staffed by the **nomenklatura** and their 'mafia' allies of old. Bureautocracies are uniquely able to emasculate policies that threaten, and mold the impact of their implementation. The Tsar's bureautocracy became, largely, the Party's; the Party's, in turn, was also essentially reincarnated, and is today democracy's.

---

[35] 'Arms and Society', *op cit.*

[36] Sources in Kiev--private; not for quotation.

Finally, the military: Under Tsars and Commissars the Army was always an integral part of the nations' leadership; the concept of coup was alien to its culture.[37] A revolutionary context, however, is by definition a time of flux, and uncertainty. In 1917 as again in 1991 the Army's conscript base and finance was ravaged, morale suffered under the onslaught of different loyalties, and some defected to causes old and new. In 1917 many followed General Alexei Brusilov's advice to stay aloof from civil strife, but be ready to answer the call when your country needs you.[38] When Poland attacked, in 1920, they followed him into the ranks of the Red Army.

Generals Boris Gromov and Alexander Lebed, the Army's most popular and charismatic 'Afghantsy' played similarly pivotal roles in 1991 and later.[39] Gromov's refusal to participate doomed the August **putsch** attempt to slow or reverse socioeconomic transformation; Lomov's protection of the Russian breakaway republic of Transdniester marked today's Polish analogue: the defence of Russia's diaspora (see chapter 5).[40]

There are of course some major **differences** between post-1917 and post-1991. The first one was the changed nature of society. Earlier Soviet society mirrored that of Tsarist Russia--peasant, poor and illiterate--; it remained governable by the same formula of authority, faith and discipline. The contemporary nation is changed: mostly urban and literate, with a genuine middle class, and contemptuous of the dogmas of the past.

The second difference lies in the new reality of a far more interconnected world, in the global nature and impact of today's information and communications technology

---

[37] Russian history resounds to memories of peasant rebellions against the established order, to names like Stenka Razin and Pugachev. Yet the Army, as an institution, always remained loyal. There were mutinies, notably the 1925 Decembrists [Guards] revolt against the accession of Nicholas l; the Petrograd garrison's defection in 1917; and the Kronstadt [Fleet] revolt of 1921, which [as Lenin said] 'lit up reality better than anything else', and led to Lenin's New Economic Policy. Yet the changes they wrought reflected the larger dynamics of which they were part; **not** the nature of their *metier*--they were **societal** agents, not military.

[38] A. Levitskii, 'General Brusilov', *Voennaia byl*, January 1968, p 19; see also David R. Jones, 'The Youth of General A.A. Brusilov: the making of the unconventional, conventional professional', address to The Royal Military College, Kingston, March 1992--and available from same.

[39] For background on Gromov, the Afghantsy and Omon networks, see **Sovinform Hypermedia on-disk** release *Soviet Military Series #1; 1989-91: Transformation & Transition*, Carleton University Soviet National Security ORU, 1991.

[40] See [eg] Stephen Foye, 'Post-Soviet Russia: Politics and the New Russian Army', *RFL/RL Research Report*, 21 August 1992; *Voennaya Mysl* special issue, July 1992; and *Nezavisimaya Gazeta*, 19 August 1992; also Chapter 5.

revolutions, and in the plug-in possibilities and potential that are inherent in the fact of an educated populace.

Third, the revolutionaries of today are not free from foreign threat. There are clearly neighbours that have actual or potential designs on former Soviet lands. Yet these threats are obviously far less immediate and acute than those faced by the **Bolsheviki**.

Fourth, however: today's revolutionaries have neither the organizational discipline nor the focused faith of the early **Bolsheviki**. Most agree on the unacceptability of the past; few agree on the definition of the future. In **lieu** of vision, greed flourishes, and undermines.[41]

The manifest relevance of political and strategic culture applies equally when considering the applicability of foreign definitions of democracy. Russian advocates of foreign economic and political prescription, and there have always been such Westernizers, have always ultimately lost out to more Slavophile arguments. This is not to say that democracy is doomed; rather, that definitions rooted in other cultures are likely to be rejected by the body politic of one that is different. Russian political culture has been dominated by authoritarianism. But it also embodies its own notions of democracy, bred by its own historical experiences and aspirations. Today's context of circumstance and hope may be uniquely propitious. But if democracy is truly to evolve, then it must be defined and shaped by and rest on these domestic roots.

---

[41] See ie 'Russia's New Code: Today, Anything Goes', *The New York Times*, 30 August 1992.

3   The Gulf War Revisited: New World Order–or Old?

ABSTRACT: The Gulf War occasioned US President Bush's proclamation of a New World Order. On closer examination, however, it is clear that Washington's prosecution and leadership of the Allied effort was grounded in and indeed determined by older tenets of American strategic culture. Perhaps more surprisingly, Moscow's acquiescence and collaboration, seen by some as a sharp departure from earlier Soviet policy, also emerges as deeply rooted in Russian foreign policy tradition. Moscow's conciliatory posture reflected temporal weakness--and traditional Soviet **and pre-Soviet** Russian response to disadvantageous power constellations in this region--, and was certainly not without precedent.

The Gulf War: Washington's War

Will history see the destruction of Saddam Hussein's armies as the dawn of George Bush's and the Allied Coalition's 'New World Order'? Or will it see a reaffirmation of a much older order--that of 1897, when British arms first 'liberated' Kuwait, severing ties to Basra and Baghdad that went back over 5000 years, and gave it independence, though not democracy, in return for financial concessions? Will it judge the novelty of collective action sanctioned by the UN Security Council, with Soviet cooperation or acquiescence, as the defining frame? Or will it emphasize rather the fact that Security Council resolutions gave legitimacy to US decisions, and the [postwar] calculation that US firms would gain most of the $100 billion business of rebuilding Kuwait?[42]

As the guns fell silent the carnage and utter one-sidedness of the 'Nintendo war' were laid bare. Over 150,000, and perhaps as many as 300,000 Iraqi soldiers dead (the exact number will never be known; reporters' video cameras showed coalition soldiers burying

---

[42] *CBC Newsworld*, 28 February 1991.

25

their foes in hastily dug, unmarked graves, apparently inundated by numbers, and fearing disease). The civilian death toll from a 'pinpoint', yet sometimes straying air-barrage that exceeded World War 2 totals, remains unknown--as does that from the ensuing civil war. And Western health officials feared even greater losses from epidemics caused by the destruction of sewage and water systems. Western forces counted their dead in tens, with perhaps half caused, inadvertently, by 'friendly fire'; of 13 British 1st Armoured Division dead, four were by Iraqi fire, nine by American.[43]

Military and technological genius clearly do not suffice to explain the contradiction between this knife-through-butter reality and the previously accepted image of Iraq's army as the world's fourth largest, steeled through victory in a brutal eight-year war with the region's former heavyweight, Iran. The image was clearly a mirage. Former US National Security Advisor Zbigniew Brzezinski's lone insistence that Iraq's military was that of a third world nation--as was Iran's--proved correct.[44]

The different image embraced by coalition officialdom was a manufactured image. Saddam was labelled Hitler, though Iraq's population of less than 17 million, its resources and ingenuity, scarcely compared with those of the Third Reich. Iraq's planes and tanks were totalled up, without regard for the fact that exceedingly few were truly modern. In the words of Canada's Richard Gwyn: 'Gigantic military hoax undid Saddam--coalition's deception meant the Iraqis never had a chance'; the deception gave Saddam the false confidence to remain in Kuwait, and magnified the glory of coalition victory.[45]

Some analysts thought the deception had deeper roots. The months before Iraq's forceful annexation of Kuwait brought numerous signals of Iraqi intent, signals clearly designed to probe for likely and possible repercussions. Iraq's immediate claims, to disputed border regions and the islands that blocked her exit to the Gulf, were emphasized, and reiterated. Kuwait's billion dollar oil extractions from Rumaila (the Iraqi oil-field that extends into disputed territory), begun while Iraq was fighting Iran, was labelled theft. Kuwait's overproduction of oil, which broke OPEC agreements and drove the price lower, jeopardizing Iraq's postwar reconstruction, was labelled hostile. Iraq's troop build up on the border was known. Yet in her final meeting with Saddam, only hours before the troops moved in, the US Ambassador gave no warning; the US empathized with Iraq's concerns, and had 'no opinion' on the question of borders.

---

[43] *Ibid*; also the *Ottawa Citizen*, 27 February 1991.

[44] See coverage from The Guardian, Le Monde and Washington Post, in the *Guardian Weekly*, 3 March 1991.

[45] The *Montreal Gazette*, 28 February 1991.

But if the United States thus in effect invited an Iraqi transgression that would justify military counteraction, the answer to the question 'why?' is neither simple, nor one-dimensional. Iraq's chemical arsenal, 'the poor man's response to (Israeli) nuclear weapons' and her efforts to acquire her own nuclear bombs, were not unique to the region. Israel's bombing of the Ozirak reactor a decade earlier had in any case demonstrated the efficacy of other alternatives. And the destruction of Iraq may spur rather than deter physically less visible pursuits of chemical arsenals--less visible, because these can be conducted in 'civilian' pharmaceutical laboratories, whereas nuclear weapons production requires visibly distinct facilities.

There is no doubt that Saddam Hussein was a ruthless thug, in a region where thuggery was the norm. Yet other regional war lords, such as Syria's Hafez Assad and Israel's Ariel Sharon had conducted 'military campaigns' that caused more civilian deaths than did Hussein's initial occupation of Kuwait; their countries remained occupiers of other lands, of larger populations, notwithstanding UN resolutions. As Western viewers watched the horror of Scuds, blazed on TV screens and front pages, others remembered the higher daily death toll of Palestinians, over weeks, months and years, a death toll obscured by intermittent, and mostly back-page coverage.

One of many ironies of this war lay in the fact that Saddam's worst atrocities were downplayed--partly, perhaps, because at the time the West had looked away. Saddam's hanging of Communist Party members from the lamp posts of Baghdad had occasioned no protest. His gassing of Kurds and Iranians during the Iraq-Iran war brought only peripheral protest, because his fight then was directed against the then 'threat-of-the-moment'--Iran's Ayatollah. It was at this time, and for this reason, that France began to supplant the USSR as Iraq's most important arms supplier, and that US, British and other arms also began to flow to Baghdad.

But if Iraq's worst atrocities were downplayed, as those of the regional thugs who joined the coalition were forgotten, others were trumpeted. Stories of incubators stolen from Kuwait, leaving babies to die, solidified support for the initial US military build up. Stories of mass rape and degradation in Kuwait City justified the launching of the air war. Stories of mass executions were seen to compel the onset of ground war.

There is no question that obscenities did occur, as they do in all wars. Yet these particular obscenities were sometimes exaggerated. Some may not have occurred. The wartime execution of Iraqi soldiers accused of rape or theft jarred with accusations that Saddam was personally responsible. The Gulf oil spill, caused in part by coalition attack, in part by Iraqi intent (to deter assault), proved one tenth as large as originally claimed.

Subsequent Western TV reports showed that the incubators had not been taken.[46] The reports also noted summary executions of Kuwaitis who had cooperated with Iraqi forces. Hate begets hate.

This was a propaganda war, on both sides. Iraqi censorship and media control was as absolute as that of the coalition military. Iraqi propaganda, cruder to the Western ear than the coalition's psy-ops--psychological operations--, though perhaps more attuned to local mindsets, was equally steeped in contradiction and irony. Saddam's regime, the most antireligious, secular and 'Westernized' of regional dictatorships (in terms of education, sexual equality and health) adopted the banner of Islam, defender of the faith, battling the onslaught of 'infidels'.

Saddam's linkage between the occupation of Kuwait and Israel's occupations of the West Bank, Gaza, and the Golan Heights was equally opportunistic. He had previously shown little regard for the plight of Palestinians, except for the sponsorship of exiled terrorist fringes who did his bidding. President Bush's dismissal of linkage was thus understandable. The refusal to countenance linkage was also unfortunate, however; a law that is not universal in principle, even if it cannot be applied simultaneously to all transgressors, invites charges of hypocrisy.

Saddam's attempts to manipulate Western opinion, by using POWs as shields, and showing evidently hurt captured pilots on TV, gave his enemies their most potent rallying cries--barbarism and torture. The prisoner shield policy was discarded, but the damage was done. The torture charge stuck until the prisoners' exchange at war's end, when the pilots testified that their facial wounds had in fact been caused by ejection.[47]

Yet there remains the nagging question of why Washington did not explore other alternatives; why Saudi security (the build-up's original objective) and Israeli security could not be safeguarded with US troops, as was Europe's during the Cold War; why sanctions were not given more time (prior to the US elections in November, CIA director W. Webster judged them 97 per cent successful; he and the President agreed they would atrophy Iraq's army, if maintained nine months or a year); why Iraq's acceptance of UN resolutions and the need to withdraw, stripped of conditions through successive Soviet mediation efforts, met categorical US rejection, and new US conditions. Regional explanations appear insufficient to warrant the scale of destruction. Moscow's lament that 'the instinct for war prevailed', when Washington ignored her plea for 24 hours to finalize Iraqi compliance, is also insufficient. The implacable rush of allied armour after it was found that Iraqi troops had

---

[46] CBC Newsworld, *op cit.*

[47] *CBC Newsworld*, 5 March 1991.

28

actually begun to withdraw before the ground onslaught began (coalition cameras recorded empty defensive lines and fortifications; the thrust up the coastal highway rolled 28 kilometres into Kuwait before catching up with the first Iraqi units) testified to a demand for victory that went well beyond the UN mandate.

Douglas Ord, a Middle East analyst, draws attention to The Revenge Factor, the US need to exorcize 'the Vietnam syndrome', the stigma of defeat and national malaise-- reinforced by the failure of President Carter's attempt to rescue hostages in Iran, the comic-opera bungling that tarred President Reagan's invasion of Grenada, and the civilian casualties wrought by 'precision bombing' during President Bush's invasion of Panama. By coincidence, the bombing of Baghdad came just after the 100th anniversary of the Massacre of Wounded Knee, where the 7th Cavalry used early rapid firing artillery to kill some 300 women and children, and 15 elderly men, while losing 25 (most, perhaps all, to friendly fire), in government-sanctioned retribution for its defeat at the Battle of the Little Bighorn 14 years earlier.[48]

Whether originally sought, whether the most potent or merely an incidental fuel for war, the exorcism of the Vietnam syndrome may prove its most lasting legacy. In the Middle East, Iraq was humiliated, and thrust into the cauldron of civil war; Iran's fundamentalists (with strong ties to Iraq's Shiite community), fomented and armed the rebellion, and hoped to profit, as did Syria and Turkey. In Kuwait, President Bush had demanded liberation, though not democracy, and that is what he and the coalition got: the emir announced martial law, and promised future elections for the enfranchised minority--though his own position would remain embedded in the constitution. The prospect of a Peace Conference to resolve the powder kegs of Palestine, and other regional passions, seen by many as the first credibility test for advocates of a new world order, remains highly uncertain.

World Order, or the hubris of vainglorious power? The former appears unlikely. History gives grounds to fear the latter.

The Gulf War: Moscow's War:
old wine in a new bottle, or new wine in an old bottle?

The end of the Cold War and a heralded, new era of Great Power cooperation, forged through summits and now war, constitutes the single most important foundation stone for the [United States] claim that a 'new world order' has been established--a world order presided over by a UN Security Council now emancipated from the schisms of the past, and

---

[48] D. Ord, 'The Revenge Factor', the *Ottawa Citizen*, 25 February 1991.

thus finally able to fulfill its original mandate. The corollary assumption is that earlier Soviet regimes would likely have vetoed UN action, and countered an American build up to defend Saudi Arabia with Red Army troops defending Baghdad (invoking Moscow's Treaty of Friendship and Cooperation with Iraq), thus ensuring and perpetuating yet another glowering stalemate. But the basic premise and the corollary assumption may both be faulty, or at least misleading. A review of Soviet policy towards the war, especially when seen against the backdrop of Soviet policy towards the Iran-Iraq war of the 1980s, suggests greater complexity, and greater uncertainty.

Soviet policy towards the unfolding crisis and the ensuing war can be quickly summarized. She supported, indeed co-sponsored every one of the twelve Security Council resolutions that sanctified the US-led Coalition's role and purpose, and that, finally, dictated the terms of Iraqi surrender. She diverted arms shipments *en route* to Iraq when Kuwait was invaded, sent Soviet naval vessels to support the UN embargo, and declared that Soviet Armed Forces ground and air units would join the coalition--if it was placed under UN command.[49] This was not accepted by Washington, which insisted on US command, and these units were [therefore] not dispatched. Nevertheless, Moscow remained supportive at all crucial decision-making junctures, and adamant that Iraq must withdraw.[50]

But Moscow also made it clear, on a number of occasions, that she would have preferred more time to consider, and perhaps pursue alternative routes to the desired end. Although Moscow always acquiesced when faced with a need to choose, she also left no question about her doubts. At every step, it was Washington that took the initiative to increase pressure, to force the confrontation, to launch the air war, and, finally, the ground war. Moscow never took any initiative that foreclosed options short of war; she maintained high-level diplomatic contact with Iraq throughout the crisis; and she launched initiatives that entertained other options. President Bush declared his 'gratitude' for [these] Soviet efforts, recognizing Moscow's need to assert and maintain a limited sphere of independent action.

Moscow initially demurred at Bush's decision after the November Congressional elections to forego sanctions in favour of an early air war, but then agreed, in return for a fifteen-day delay (from 1 January to 15 January). When Moscow's final peace initiative secured Iraq's agreement to withdraw, and sufficiently specific Iraqi agreement to comply with other UN resolutions to gain explicit acceptance from Italy's Prime Minister, and

---

[49] R. Weitz, 'The USSR and the Confrontation in the Gulf', *RFE/RL Report on the USSR*, 17 August 1990, pp 1-2. Soviet merchant ships [also] helped transport US forces and equipment; see *International Defence Review*, February 1991.

[50] *New York Times*, 25 February 1991, p 1.

30

implicit acceptance from other NATO governments and officials, however, Washington would not be deterred; Moscow bemoaned 'the instinct for war' (with Iraqi withdrawal begun, the United States 'could have waited a day or two'), but accepted the decision.[51]

Moscow's cooperation was generally ascribed to Gorbachev's 'new thinking', his de-ideologization of Soviet foreign policy, and his reliance on Western partners to help alleviate Soviet economic problems. His occasional demonstration of inquietude, was deemed to reflect the concerns of the Soviet Union's more than 40 million Muslims, and the need to mollify conservative Party and Army officials upset at the 'betrayal' of an old ally. The more forceful peace initiative of the war's final days was ascribed to the need to appease a third, growing 'oppositional' force--the wider constituency of pragmatic nationalists, who feared that events would lead to a permanent US presence in the region, and/or to dismemberment of Iraq and a more potent [still fundamentalist] Iran.

The explicitness of Moscow's bottom-line acquiescence probably did reflect Moscow's new course; Moscow's endorsement of UN action and command mirrored one of the major themes of Gorbachevian foreign policy; the attributed reasons for circumspection and some flaunting of independent initiative were clearly pertinent. The more startling point is that this policy was in fact not very different from that pursued by other, previous Soviet (and Russian) regimes.

Moscow's Treaty of Friendship and Cooperation with Iraq never reflected ideological kinship--a fact confirmed by Saddam Hussein's murderous decimation of Iraq's Communist Party (before and after the signing of the Treaty, in 1972). It was quintessential *real-politik*, reflecting the same geopolitical considerations that fuelled earlier and later Western courtship of Iraq. A strong Iraq blunted Iran's regional power ambitions, balanced Syria's pan-Arab dreams, and countered NATO Turkey--as did Syria, Moscow's other 'ally'. Moscow's first consideration was the security of her southern borders, and regions. In the 19th Century she lent arms (and armies) to Balkan separatism and proffered 'protection' of the Holy Land, to weaken the Ottoman Empire, and ward off other claimants. In this Century she has moved to counter the ascendancy of all would-be regional powers--and subversive theologies.

Soviet intervention in Afghanistan was in part the visceral response of a great power facing the loss of a strategic buffer and an historic dominance [in northern Afghanistan] that dated back more than 150 years. It was also in part designed to block the aspirations of ascendant Iran, and the subversive potential of [its] Islamic fundamentalism.[52] The initial

---

[51] V. Ostrovsky, 'US Has Other Aims', *Novosti*, 27 February 1991.

[52] M. Urban, *War in Afghanistan*, London: Macmillan, 1988, p 206.

success of Iraq's invasion of Iran in 1982 shifted the focus of greatest concern. Moscow stopped arms deliveries to Baghdad, and urged Iraqi withdrawal.[53]

Moscow's policy was essentially the same as England's old policy towards continental Europe--to support those who would blunt the ambitions of others, to ensure that no one nation (and potential rival) become too strong. Moscow also sought to avert intrusions into the region by other great powers. But, recognizing the limitations of her armies and logistics, neither Tsarist Russia nor the Soviet Union has felt able to challenge such incursions directly.

Challenges have been indirect, through [often surreptitious] support to local and regional opposition to such incursions, support that did not commit Moscow directly. From her acceptance of Britain's ultimatum before to the Crimean War, to her withdrawal from northwestern Iran and from putative involvement in the Greek Civil War after World War 2, Moscow shied away from direct challenge, foregoing established interests and gain. When offered the choice (and this fact is equally relevant to considerations of the above corollary assumption of a Soviet alternative), Moscow's first option has always been to try to co-opt and thus dilute the ramifications of outside power intrusions into the region.

When Britain appeared ready to challenge and dismember a weakened Ottoman Empire, Russia tried to forge an alliance. In 1941 she joined the British invasion of Iran. In 1984, as Iraq's armies were forced to relinquish most of their initial gains, and Western arms flowed into Baghdad, she resumed her own arms deliveries to Iraq--though these were now balanced by arms sales also to Iran. When the war threatened Gulf oil deliveries, she joined the US-led re-flagging effort; three Kuwaiti oil tankers were given Soviet protection. When Iran finally broke the stalemate and occupied the Faw peninsula, precipitating a sharp increase in Western arms support to Iraq, the flow of Soviet arms to Baghdad rose even more dramatically. But, again, it is important to note that this was not merely a competitive response, aimed at offsetting influence. The orchestration of arms and advice to Iraq and other pressures on Iran that forced Iranian withdrawal and cease-fire showed extensive, *de facto* US-Soviet cooperation and coordination.[54]

The fact of US-Soviet cooperation and coordination in the Gulf War to evict Iraq from Kuwait was thus not in itself either novel or surprising, once President Bush committed The United States to action. Action against Iraqi aggrandizement accorded with the

---

[53] Three recipients of Soviet arms, Egypt, Somalia and North Yemen, continued shipments to Iraq; these were [now] 'balanced' by shipments to Iran from three others, Syria, Libya and North Korea.

[54] Mohiaddin Mesbahi, 'Soviet Policy towards the Iran-Iraq War', in C.G. Jacobsen, ed., *Soviet Foreign Policy; New Dynamics, New Themes*, London and New York: Macmillan and St. Martin's Press, 1989, pp 163-181.

traditions of Russian and Soviet policy; so did the (in this case reinforcing) decision not to directly oppose US intervention. On the other hand, Moscow's formal support for the 'Coalition', as well as the veiled dissonance of Soviet initiatives towards the end of the conflict, both reflected the fact and continuing relevance of other, distinct Russian/Soviet policy imperatives. The most important of these are clearly the desire to circumscribe longer-term US influence, and to undermine pretexts for a more permanent US armed presence, or base. The latter, in particular, would obviously have been more difficult to deny if US action had been unilateral, or if the eviction of Iraq from Kuwait was to be followed up by a peace so punitive that it threatened Iraq's internal stability, and therefore also its ability to fulfill its assigned role in the regional power equation. The sweep of the final ground offensive and the outbreak of civil war that followed (sparked by President Bush's calls for the overthrow of Saddam Hussein, and fuelled by Iran's arms and ambition) put the spectre in sharp relief; by March there was talk of permanent US basing facilities in Bahrain.

In the context of domestic turmoil, and her own inability to dictate events, Moscow may yet find such basing opportune, if it helps thwart Iran's attempts to exploit Iraqi weakness (and annex its Shiite south), and if the Oslo Accord that superceded the US/Soviet-sponsored Peace Conference can resolve some of the Palestinian and other problems that perennially de-stabilize the region, and thus serve [also] other Russian interests.

Yet Moscow's interests in the region remain distinctly different from those of the United States. The region may be crucial to US energy security, in the absence of effective domestic energy conservation and/or alternative energy policies. Its importance to Moscow, however, transcends the vicissitudes of domestic politics; rather, it is a function of geographic proximity and enduring security concern. Its sensitivity to Moscow was perhaps best expressed in former Secretary General Yuri Andropov's then-startling suggestion that US interventionary policies in Central America might be as legitimate as Moscow's need to intervene in Afghanistan--to the extent that they derived from analogous considerations of geopolitical *diktat*.[55] He proceeded to weaken the analogy's applicability to Nicaragua, by noting its very considerable distance from US borders. Nevertheless, the analogy well suggests the immediacy and visceral nature of Moscow's concerns. It heralded Moscow's withdrawal from confrontational policies in Central America, and later from other conflict arenas where the marginality of possible Soviet security benefits were judged to be not worth the cost. It also graphically confirms that Moscow does not see the Middle East as [such] a region of marginal impact; to the contrary, it sees it as vital to its wider security interests.

---

[55] Interview with General Secretary Yuri Andropov, *Der Spiegel*, 19 April 1983; and *Tass*, 24 April 1983.

In this context the uncertain ramifications of 'the military lesson' must also be noted. The defeated army had much Soviet weaponry, but most was old, and the best flew to Iran; the antique Scud barely hints at the potency of superpower arsenals. Since Marshal Ogarkov's appointment as Chief of the General Staff in 1977, modern Soviet arms development has (also) focused increasingly on new and exotic technologies; Iraq's defeat says as little about Soviet power as American-armed General Manuel Noriega's said about US power.[56] The course of the war did not undermine the Soviet armed forces' chosen developmental path; it confirmed it. It may, however, have undermined Moscow's newer defensive defence doctrine, and prospects for further cuts in the military budget. Soviet military comment echoed Ogarkov's old insistence that new technology potentials compel ever-increasing flexibility, rapid-thrust combined-arms forward(!) mobility--and increased investment.[57] [A parallel argument led to an increase in China's military budget, within weeks of the end of the Gulf War.]

A New World Order? Gorbachev's embrace of [the Palme Commission's] concept of mutual security, and collective security through the UN--reflected in Moscow's payment of past dues and support for the Gulf operation--, appeared responsive. The triumphant unilateralism and UN neglect of postwar American commentary--reflected also in the fact that still-unpaid US dues exceed total dues owed by all other members--, does not; it flaunts national purpose, not collective action. But then calls for new world orders have always reflected *national* aspirations. And history may judge Gorbachev little different. His embrace of new visions and extraordinary willingness to discard at least some of the shibboleths of national dogma, have propelled extraordinary change, yet they too, surely, rest on perceptions of *national* need, and purpose. The concept of mutual security may yet transcend exclusive manifestations of (such) national will and purpose, if embedded in national psyches and cultures. The Gulf War may not have served that purpose--either in Moscow, or further afield.

---

[56] For detailed, comparative analyses, see C.G. Jacobsen, ed., *Strategic Power: USA/USSR*, London and New York: Macmillan and St. Martin's Press, 1990.

[57] See especially Marshal of the Tank Armies O. Losik's review in *Krasnaya Zvezda*, 5 March 1991. For a good summary article in English, see the *Christian Science Monitor*, 23 March 1991. Others [reform officers] saw occasion to renew calls for 'professional', non-conscript forces: see Major N. Pogorelny's cautious 'What the War Showed', in *Krasnaya Zvezda*, 8 March 1991; and Soviet Press Review, *Jane's Soviet Intelligence Review*, 19 March 1991.

The Gulf War Theatre

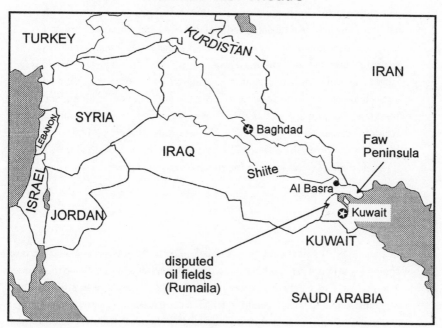

4 Yugoslavia's Wars of Secession and Succession

ABSTRACT: The lands of the Southern Slavs, history's fault line between Rome and Byzantium, Catholicism and Orthodoxy, Christianity and Islam, have again erupted. Such eruptions have always reflected and spawned myth and bias, mirroring the different agendas of domestic and external actors. Yet the latest conflagration set a new standard. Propaganda and outside interests defined its outbreak and course, skewering evidence, and judgement. Tito's Yugoslavia defied Moscow, spurned Washington, and charted and chartered Non-Alignment, as the most successful opt-out of the Era of Confrontation. Its sequel, as primary victim of the new and different confrontational dynamics unleashed by the ending of that era, constitutes one of history's most poignant reversals of fate. It also helps define the New World Order's older and darker essence, adding larger-canvas tragedy to cruel irony.

Background; the weight of history

The lands that were Yugoslavia, the lands of the Southern Slavs, have straddled the front lines of competing civilizations, cultures, religions and empires since the dawn of recorded history. The roots of Croat-Serb differences reflect Croatia's emergence from Rome's and Attila's domains, while most Serb lands remained under Byzantium's sway; their legacy is echoed in Croatia's Catholicism and Roman alphabet, in Serbia's Eastern Orthodoxy and Cyrillic script. The briefly independent Croatia of the 10th and 11th centuries (it was conquered by Hungary) extended from the primary Croat lands West of the Cetina river to the Dalmatian territories of their Orthodox cousins--the secessionist Serb Krajina state of 1991-95.[58] The Serb state Rascia, established in the mountains of Bosnia, subsequently expanded to incorporate most Serb lands and dominate the Balkans, until its defeat by the northward thrusting Ottoman Empire in 1389, at the battle of Kosovo Polje. The defeat's

---

[58] The first chronicle to describe these lands as Serb is that of the Frankish scholar Ainhard, in 822.

36

mythology would ultimately be nation-defining (serving much the same role as the Alamo in American culture).

Through the next centuries, however, Serb lands would remain the provinces of others, with 'Vojna Krajina' designated a distinct Austro-Hungarian frontier zone, while Bosnia, its Croatian/Catholic sub-component Herzegovina, and 'Serbia' became Ottoman domains, until, when that Empire began to crumble following the Russo-Turkish war of 1877-78, Vienna extended its sway to Bosnia, and Serbia won independence. Serb-Muslim and less immediate Croat-Muslim differences are an Ottoman legacy: entry in the civil service and most professions required conversion to Islam; hence the Muslims' urban concentration, and the far more extensive land-holdings of the farming, Orthodox Serbs.[59]

The first harbinger of contemporary horrors was Austro-Hungary's revenge against the assassination of the Arch-Duke Ferdinand by a Serb gunman in Sarajevo in 1914, the precipitating event of World War 1. Croatian units of the Austro-Hungarian army committed extensive massacres of Serb civilians (the first 'genocide').[60]

There were also Croats who contributed to a different legacy. Croat intellectuals were in the forefront of those who championed Yugoslavia as a South Slav confederacy, a coming together of long-separated family, upon the defeat and breakup of Austro-Hungary in 1918. But the darker legacy festered. It provided rationale for what others saw as Serb perversion of the vision; Belgrade's chauvinist memories, slanted by recent victimization, religious and cultural prejudice drove dynamics that transformed the confederacy into an orthodox/nationalist Greater Serbia.

With World War 2 the pendulum swung back, viciously. The invading German army identified Serbia and the larger Serb population as its primary enemy; their consequent strategy was to divide and split Serb lands. 11th century Croatia was recreated, with Krajina a component part, with an **Ustasha** Nazi party clone and a mini-Fuhrer, Ante Pavelic (its promulgation was flanked by pictures of Adolf Hitler and Benito Mussolini). Bosnia remained a separate entity, acknowledged as Serb, but was detached from Yugoslavia, and given to Croatia. Kosovo, to the south, was also detached--its Serb ethnicity diluted through expulsion of about 200,000 Serbs, and importation of over 300,000 Muslims from Italian-occupied Albania. With extraordinary support from the Catholic clergy (perhaps the most

---

[59] *Karta Nashchikh Pobedela / Maps of Our Dividings; political atlas of Yugoslav countries in the XX Century*, Belgrade: BMG [independent/Academy], 1991, provides historical 20th Century territorial claim and population distribution maps for all former Yugoslav lands. Re Bosnia, specifically, see also *Territorial Distribution of Serbs in Bosnia and Herzegovina*, Belgrade: [University] Faculty of Geography, 1992.

[60] R.A. Reiss, *Report Upon the Atrocities Committed by the Austro-Hungarian Army During the First Invasion of Serbia*, London: Simkin, Marshall, Hamilton, Kent & Co., 1916.

nefarious chapter in Catholic Church history) the Pavelic/Ustasha regime established work and extermination camps--most notoriously Jasenovac--for Jews and Serb *unter-menschen*.[61] In Bosnia their round-ups were led by the infamous Hanjar SS division, consecrated by the Mufti of Jerusalem (with another such division that fought on the Eastern Front) in return for Hitler-promised postwar favours; Sarajevo was Europe's first **Judenfrei** city.[62] After the war the Nuremberg tribunal rendered formal genocide judgement against Croatia.

Serb resistance initially rallied around the ethnic/chauvinist Chetnik banner, yet the Chetniks' embrace of the royalist past drove many, and also, ultimately, Western aid, to Broz Tito's pan-national, communist partisans, who prevailed after what was in effect a civil war within a war of national resistance, and survival. Tito's Croat ethnicity helped recruit anti-Nazi, anti-Pavelic Croats and Muslims, though orthodox Serbs remained predominant within the movement, in both absolute and (with Jewish Serbs) relative numbers.

Croat, Muslim and other minority representation remained a prominent characteristic of the usually though not always benign dictatorship established by Tito's Communist Party of Yugoslavia after the war. Thus Army and Interior Ministry Security Services, for example, remained largely under Croat leadership until the final demise of the union; later Croat President Franjo Tudjman first saw prominence as their youngest General--and Tito protege. Serb lands remained divided. Administrative divisions perpetuated larger Croatia and Bosnia (as orthodox outmigrations in the late 1960s made Muslims, for the first time, the slightly larger Bosnian group, they were also, for the first time, given distinct 'national' status), and gave autonomous province designations to Serbia's Kosovo and northern Voivodina--with its Hungarian minority concentration.

His battles with the Chetniks taught Tito too that a united, nationalist Serbia constituted the greatest danger to other control designs. But his background also made him sensitive to the minority alienation that would attend Serb satisfaction. He may have assumed that Serb pride could in any case be assuaged by their inevitable numeric dominance of most central organs. He certainly expected a transcendent Yugoslav identification to make such issues moot in the long run. In the interim, wartime horrors were assigned to history: victim memorials remembered crimes rather than ethnicities; horrors

---

[61] Hori Broszat, *Der Kroatische Ustasche*, Stuttgart: Staatinstitut fur Zeitgeschichte, 1965; see also i.e. *Report of SS Gruppenfuhrer Turner to the Military Commander for the Southeast*, 3 September 1941; acts of the personal staff of SS Reichsfuhrer Himmler, 651866, p 328.

[62] Joseph Lapid, 'They shared our fate', *The Jerusalem Post*, 4 February 1994; John Ranz, 'Serbs, Jews and Bosnia', *Jewish Week*, 5-11 August 1994; also Hinko Gotlieb, 'Kaddish in the Serbian Forest', *The Massacre of European Jewry*, pp 307-8 (available from Buchenwald Survivors, Brooklyn, New York)

were of the past--there would be no revanchism, no restitution; security forces were directed to act against any and all manifestations of ethno-nationalism.

A Yugoslav identity did indeed appear ascendant after the war. Tito's Balkan aspirations (though ultimately thwarted), his defiance of Stalin and forging of Non-Alignment reflected an international role that most took pride in. Domestically the early transition to a relatively free-market economy and liberalization of travel and currency regulations (which led to significant **gast-arbeiter** remittances from West Germany) spurred sufficient development to allow both local growth and subsidizing transfers to poorer regions. Both pillars of this relative-contentment formula frayed after Tito's death.

The convoluted successor arrangement, a collegium presidency, with the *pro forma* title rotated annually between regional leaders, proved a recipe for grid-lock. Designed to enshrine ethnic harmony, it instead exacerbated discord. Serbs demanded more equitable power sharing, giving them authority proportionate to their numbers. Smaller groups, especially those more developed, sought decentralization and autonomy. Neither found satisfaction.

European growth contraction cut **gast-arbeiter** positions and remittances, worsening Yugoslavia's own descent into stagnation and debt. Equalization payments required of richer Slovenia and Croatia began to hurt more, as demands from less developed regions (including Serbia) became more acute. The contradiction fuelled the arguments of Slovenian and Croat separatists and Serb centralizers alike.

With the growth redistribution pie gone other building blocks of Tito's pan-national aspiration became fodder instead for ethnic discord. The most dramatic example was Kosovo, where wartime German relocations were followed by further growth in Muslim numbers; they were swelled by refugees from Enver Hoxha's more repressive Albania, and higher birth rates. This set the stage for Muslim separatism (encouraged and supported by both Albanian irredentists and fundamentalist guardians) and Serb paranoia. Thus Serb leader Slobodan Milosovic' forceful 1989 Kosovo Polje anniversary speech celebrating Serb culture and rights, and his government's decision to revoke Kosovo's and Voivodina's autonomy (while promising protection for minority rights). Thus also Serb reactions to then President Bush's 1991 support for Kosovo Muslims' separatist aspirations--which mirrored what American reaction would be to an outside power demanding special rights for the majority Mexican population around the Alamo.

Milosevic' 1989 speech is sometimes portrayed as the first embrace of ethno-nationalism. Yet it was as much a response as a spark. Franjo Tudjman had pursued his alternative constituency of Croat chauvinism ever since Tito dismissed him; through the mid and late 1980s his speeches and articles developed the themes of Nazi and Ustasha exculpation that infused his later book, *Wasteland*--which dismissed the holocaust, and, indeed, blamed supposedly Jewish prison guards for Jewish deaths.[63]

Alija Izetbegovic had also long nurtured an alternate constituency, developing ties with Ayatollah Khomenei's Iran; his *Islamic Declaration*, a fundamentalist clarion call that designated Islam the ultimate and all-affecting self- and state identifier, was first published in 1970.[64]

Recognitions; 'inviolate borders'; Serbs as outcasts

The 1991-92 rush to recognize the independence of former constituent republics of Yugoslavia and the USSR within their existing boundaries was perceived by many as a moral imperative. For that reason obstacles of international and national law were also set aside. To some extent, in both cases, the haste was a post Cold War yet quintessentially Cold War reflex, assuming the democratic credentials of anti-'Communist' dissidents. In Yugoslavia's case these assumptions were further reinforced by an extraordinarily well funded Croatian PR campaign that effectively set the moral tone and agenda--though more pragmatic reasons of **real-politik** lurked beneath the surface (see below).

The recognitions of Slovenia, Croatia, Bosnia and Macedonia were startling in that they contravened most of the recognizing countries' own rules for recognition. The new states did not have uncontested control of their territories; in some cases minority-dominated and at least some other regions clearly opposed independence; all the recognitions contravened the stipulations of the Helsinki Accords that sanctified postwar European boundaries--and stipulated that these could be changed only with the consent of affected state actors (ie Yugoslavia in this case).

Slovene, Croat and selected others were granted self-determination as a natural right. Yet the international community had previously been unwilling to concede such rights to other minority ethnic populations. Since fighting its own Civil War to deny secession the United States had consistently opposed secessionist aspirations elsewhere, even where these enjoyed obvious public support--as had others. Thus none recognized the Ibos' state of

---

[63] F. Tudjman, *Wasteland*, Zagreb: Matica Hrvatska Publishing Institute, 1990.

[64] On Alija Izetbegovic' **fundamentalist** equation of identity and religion (initially not shared by most Bosnian Muslims, who traditionally were the most secular of Bosnia's three communities), and his ties with the Ayatollah's regime, see *Iran's European Springboard*, Task Force on Terrorism & Unconventional Warfare, House Republican Research Committee, US House of Representatives, Washington DC, 1 September 1992; and Izetbegovic' *The Islamic Declaration*, Sarajevo: Muslim **samizdat**, 1970--reprinted 1990.

Biafra when it attempted to secede from Nigeria; none recognized Katanga when it tried to break from the Congo.

The recognition of secessionist states' former, internal administrative borders, now declared 'inviolate', meant, *ipso facto* that the right to self-determination was not extended to **their** minorities. Disastrously, this ignored the ramifications of these borders' origin. In Yugoslavia as in the Soviet Union they were not congruent with ethnic space. They were drawn to satisfy the sometimes arbitrary policy options and agendas of the respective dictatorships. In some cases they incorporated parts of one or more ethnic groups within another's *pro forma* space precisely so as to thwart secessionist ambitions (as in Croatia, Bosnia and Soviet Georgia); in others they did the same to buy whoever's allegiance was less certain (as when Stalin gave Armenian Nagorno-Karabakh to Azerbaijan), as compensation for perceived loss or suffering (as when Stalin gave Vilnius and other lands to Lithuania after its annexation in 1939), or as reward for personal loyalty (as when Khrushchev gave the Crimea to Ukraine in 1954 without even the fig-leaf of constitutionally required Supreme Soviet assent). Clearly, and as subsequent history confirmed, many of these borders were borders whose recognition would prescribe war rather than peace.[65]

This was particularly true in Croatia, especially under the circumstances of 1990-92. Croatian Serbs had no need of Belgrade propaganda. Their worst fears were confirmed by Tudjman's adoption or encouragement of **Ustasha** insignia, songs and legends; by the suspension of police and judicial authorities in districts that voted against Tudjman in 1990; the promulgation of a draft constitution that conspicuously omitted Serbs from its list of protected minorities (Western pressure forced amendment, but by then it was too late); the publication of a 'black book', actually pale blue, that listed Serb family names in Western Slavonia, much as Germany and Egypt once marked Jewish doors; and the first ethnic cleansings, ordered by Croat commanders--which sparked and fuelled the ensuing civil war, and Krajina's declared secession.[66] As previously noted by this author, and others: to expect

---

[65] C.G. Jacobsen, 'On the Search for a New World Security Order: 'The Inviolability of Borders'; Prescription for Peace or War?', *European Security*, Spring 1992.

[66] Vukovar was one city where Tudjman 'commissars' (later among the first accused of war crimes) replaced locally elected officials, after an estimated 80% of its and surrounding areas' Croat populations voted with Serb opponents in the 1990 elections that brought Tudjman to power. The first ethnic cleansings are documented in *Helsinki Watch Letter to Franjo Tudjman, President of the Republic of Croatia*, Washington and New York: Helsinki Watch, 13 February 1992. The 'black book': *Tke je Tko u Daruvaru*, Zagreb: Tiskara 'Ognjen Prica' Daruvar, January 1992; see also Mila Lucic, *L'Extermination des Serbes*, Novi Sad: Musee Historique de Voivodine, 1991.

Serbs to accept this Croatia's sovereignty was like expecting Warsaw Ghetto survivors to accept a Germany that hoisted Nazi symbols--it made war inevitable.[67]

It would also be true in Bosnia. The 15 October 1991 Bosnian Assembly Muslim-Croat vote for independence saw Serb walk-out, followed by a Serb referendum that voted overwhelmingly for Yugoslav affiliation. The consequent illegality of the breakaway decision (Bosnia's constitution stipulated inter-ethnic agreement as precondition for change) was ignored by its champions. Nevertheless, an unquantifiable but significant portion of the Serb population and leadership, evincing inculcated Yugoslav non-nationalism, responding to the bloodshed unfolding in Croatia and Western urging, and confident in the Muslim majority's secular credentials, was initially willing to support or acquiesce in the momentum to independence.

The acquiescence evaporated when Izetbegovic withdrew his signature from the Lord Carrington brokered Lisbon agreement of 19 March 1992 that divided Bosnia into three ethnic cantons; he did so five days later, upon the urging of US Ambassador Warren Zimmerman. Izetbegovic' subsequent acceptance of an Iranian-sponsored Mojaheddin contingent from Lebanon, employed in under-reported preemptive Muslim offensives against Serb communities in eastern Bosnia and against northeastern Bijeljina, 'confirmed' and massively reinforced more paranoid Serb views. Now unleashed, the war option became the only option.

Warren Zimmerman later reconsidered: the intervention was his 'greatest mistake'.[68] The US State Department official who subsequently resigned (followed by others) in a blaze of publicity, demanding **more** vigorous support for Izetbegovic, would also reconsider; he had been wrong: Izetbegovic' 'government' was in fact a 'clique of nationalist politicians...inexperienced, corrupt'.[69] So would James Baker, the Secretary of State who sponsored the original recognitions: in January 1995 he bemoaned the acceptance of

---

[67] C.G. Jacobsen, 'War Crimes in the Balkans: media manipulation, historical amnesia and subjective morality', *Coexistence*, Glasgow and Amsterdam, no. 30 1993 (for an elaborated version, see 'Yugoslavia's Wars of Succession', *Mediterranean Quarterly*, Washington DC, August 1994); the Jewish analogy was echoed ie by Henry Kissinger, in a May 1993 interview on ABC television. Note also Henry Kissinger's statements to the *Los Angeles Times*, 16 May 1993.

[68] David Binder, 'US Policymakers on Bosnia Admit Errors in Opposing Partition in 1992', *The New York Times*, 29 August 1993.

[69] George Kenney, 'Ending Bosnia's Endgame', *The New York Times*, 1 December 1994.

Yugoslav dismemberment--and acknowledged that it was Slovene and Croatian use of 'force to seize their border posts...that, indeed, triggered the civil conflict...'[70]

Yet the Zimmerman intervention was but the first of a pattern of US interventions to shore up the Izetbegovic government's will and combat ability, and effectively sabotage occasional European, UN [and former President Carter's December 1994] attempts to explore compromise solutions--and, in essence, resuscitate the Carrington formula. Washington's forceful posture, epitomized by covert military advisory aid prior to the Muslim 5th Corp's offensive out of Bihac in the fall of 1994 and the government's March 1995 attacks towards the Serb 'corridor', out of Tuzla, as well as by sponsorship of NATO air-strikes against Serbs and threats to exempt the Muslim government from the UN arms embargo on all belligerents, clearly perpetuated the conflicts ravaging Bosnia. It also responded to and found justification in the generally accepted theme of Serb culpability. As will be seen, the selective manufacturing and gross exaggeration of this theme in fact undercut its moral authority, jeopardizing both war crime prosecution and historic judgement. The contrived moral parameters and the question of more pragmatic, underlying interests of geopolitics and economic advantage are both addressed below.

But there is one other aspect of the legalization of Yugoslav (and Soviet) dismemberment that deserves attention. It was not merely aberrational in terms of previously developed strictures of international law. It was also consigned to remain aberrational by the subsequent evolution of these strictures--*viz* later attitudes towards the separatist Parti Québécois of Canada's Quebec province. Quebec, of course, was and is a close analogue to Croatia: its deeply split French majority coexists not just with more committed federalist Anglo and immigrant communities (who with French federalists may be seen as Canada's 'Yugoslavs'), but also with homogeneous Aboriginal groups that constitute clear majorities within their regions.

Following the PQ's 1994 Provincial election victory, on a platform that promised an independence referendum, Ottawa pointedly referred to international legal opinion that granted automatic self determination rights only to colonized peoples, not to components of democratic states, however distinct. Ottawa proceeded to declare that in the unforeseen circumstance of a clear French majority vote to secede, the right to do so, if nevertheless granted, must also be extended to a then-likely similarly expressed preference on the part of, for example, Quebec's northern Cree community. The Party Québécois' contrary position received no support from the governments that once conceded Zagreb's similar stand. To the contrary, as evidenced for example in the positions taken by US President Clinton during his

---

[70] James Baker, testimony, Hearings before the House International Relations Committee, 12 January 1995, *Congressional Record*, Washington DC: GPO, 1995.

early 1995 visit to Ottawa, the United States and the international community in general seemed clearly to have reverted to their pre-1991 views.

'All that's fit to print'; the setting of moral parameters; the reasons

Historically, war blame and crime designations mirror particular interests. There are contexts such as Buchenwald or Jasenovac where crimes may be said to transcend interests and compel judgement. But attempts to cast the Yugoslav successor wars as such a context have, as shown below, been too contrived to convince. One must therefore seek other rationales.

In Yugoslavia one preponderant US and European interest was to placate and integrate united Germany, Croatia's sponsor. Thus the Bush administration's embrace of the recognition option came only after it became clear that the European Community was determined to proceed; it was clearly motivated at least partly by the desire not to be out of step. The European Community also was initially disinclined: Germany's recognition advocacy was at first supported by only two other governments; the rest, including London and Paris, acquiesced only after German pressure, and concessions on the Maastricht Treaty --the European Union next step that was then being negotiated.

The other preponderant, primarily US interest, was to nurture Muslim ties, to meet the charge that Baghdad was bombed because it was Muslim (would we do the same to a Christian 'outlaw'?), to protect astronomical Kuwaiti and other contracts (Kuwaiti reconstruction contracts alone totalled over $100 billion), safeguard oil interests, and, not least, to counter fundamentalist Iran. The latter concerns also dictated support for those whose very fear of Iran (the Kuwaitis, Saudis and Benazir Bhutto) compelled embrace of pan-Islam's new defining banner; with Palestinian plight on the back burner because of the ongoing peace process, Bosnia's Muslims became the *cause celebre* of the Islamic world. As Turkey scrambled to counter Teheran's attempted end run into its former dominion another escalatory factor was added. Still, while consequent pressures on US and other western interests thus drew nurture also from older Middle East rivalries, the primary dynamic clearly had its roots in the Gulf War. The Gulf War definition of the 'New World Order' set the geopolitical parameters that determined interests in Bosnia.

But interests must still have moral cloak. In this case, moral parameters were set by Croatia's extraordinarily successful PR campaign. Their preemptive investment was eye-popping; on some US and Canadian TV stations they outspent Coke and Pepsi combined.[71] It was worth it. Two millennia ago the Chinese sage Sun Tsu noted that the finest victory was the one won without loss of life. The Croats learned from Kuwait--the nurse's Congressional testimony about babies torn from incubators sent to Baghdad, front-paged by the *New York Times* and featured on every TV screen, was later exposed as false, but by then the war it fuelled was long over (she was the daughter of Kuwait's Washington Ambassador; the incubators, with healthy babies, were there at war's end; the falsehood was spread by Wall Street's largest PR firm, Ruder Finn). Croatia engaged Ruder Finn. Once again deliberately manufactured and provided falsehoods were featured by the *New York Times* and others (see below), with contrary evidence often suppressed, by minds already set.

Croatia's nationalists had in fact declared war. And they very nearly achieved Sun Tsu's ideal. They set the war's parameters and historical context. Both were further reinforced when Islamic and US contributions allowed the Izetbegovic government to launch its own Wall Street campaign, in 1993 (the Belgrade government secured its own US PR outlet in 1994, though at far lower funding levels; Krajina and Srbska--the Bosnian Serb state--governments remained unable to follow suit, for both political and fiscal reasons).

Conflict participants' one-sided presentations of horrors are, of course, not exceptional. And the daily arrival of faxes from Ruder Finn to *New York Times'* and others' journalists in the field and at head offices might be expected to have some impact. Nevertheless, their apparent disinterest in seeking out a more balanced overview of the totality of horrors--for civil wars are never one-sided (see below)--was exceptional. This would belie, or at least severely jeopardize consequent moral judgement; it also bespoke the fact of other interests.

Documentation of deliberate bias is extensive. Trade embargo and sanctions against Serbia was presented as punishment for the Yugoslav army's involvement in Bosnia, though a UN report confirmed its withdrawal to Serbia (the report's release was withheld until after the Security Council vote). The continuing presence in Bosnia of Croatian military units occasioned no protest.

The sanctions devastated Serb civilian industry, the poor and refugees; dialysis machines and other hospital equipment ceased to function; medicines and diapers disappeared. They did little damage to Serb military potential (their inherited military industry was uniquely self-sufficient), or to the elite. Far from rallying opposition to Milosovic, the sanctions in fact reaffirmed the Serb 'Massada complex', and fuelled the electoral success of harder, nationalist parties. They destroyed the legitimacy and arguments

---

[71] This reflects relative time allotted to [their] respective advertisement on three channels monitored by the ICWCB, and assumes equal advertisement-time costs.

of Milosevic' democratic pro-Western opposition, and gave primary opposition status instead to Serb neo-fascism. The fundamentalist dynamic that had perverted Croat and Muslim cultures was now ensconced in Serbia also. Western media evinced scant reflection.

The theme of Serb military preponderance was itself misleading. Tito had prepared Yugoslavia for a People's War against a worst-case Soviet invasion contingency. This included population-wide training, Vietnam-modelled tunnelling complexes under cities and some countryside, and extraordinarily extensive, dispersed arms caches designed to guarantee all localities the ability to perpetuate resistance even when cut off from other parts of the country.

During the initial stages of war, in Slovenia briefly, and then Croatia, the new nationalist militias were furthermore often better organized and always more cohesive. The Yugoslav Army was a multiethnic army, under multiethnic command; as individuals and whole units defected to the new formations it was confused and crippled. Through the Croatian campaigns, including the final storming of Vukovar, it was in fact the now mushrooming Serb militias (or **freikorps**) that most effectively engaged in battle.[72]

The theme of Bosnian Muslim military paucity, later trumpeted by some US Congressmen as well as the media, was similarly ignorant--or disingenuous. Aside from the fact of well-stocked depots, the Bosnian Muslim space always contained more of Bosnia's former Yugoslav military industries than did Srbska; many of these were furthermore located in the UN-designated 'safe havens', which fact explains why most Muslim offensives have struck out from **them**. The Yugoslav inheritance was of course considerably enhanced by covert US, Iranian and other-source deliveries through the Winter, Spring and Summer of 1995 (see below).

The spectre that long deterred substantive Western escalation, that of all-out involvement of the now cohesive Serbianized Yugoslav army, would have involved forces of another order. With that Army on the sidelines, however, Srbska's arms advantage underwhelmed even prior to 1995. It is noteworthy that while the *New York Times* and others proclaimed dire Muslim shortages, British, Canadian and other UN contingents' daily military briefings documented the greater frequency of **Muslim** offensives.[73] Srbska's artillery inheritance from the former federal Army was in most cases singularly irrelevant;

---

[72] Arkan's Tigers led the final assault on Vukovar. Interviewed by the ICWCB in Belgrade, in February 1993, Arkan was both dismissive and derisive concerning the role played by the federal Army; ICWCB archives, Ottawa.

[73] Thus *HQ BRITFOR - CURRENT SITUATION MAP*, 27 June 1994 (the chance first-draw from ICWCB archives, and typical of the time) shows five outward arrows of 'Muslim Activity'; none of 'Serbian Activity'; none of 'Croatian Activity'.

former UN Commander General Lewis Mackenzie argued that it rewarded cowardice more often than it affected combat (the safety of distance encouraged more Slivovic drinking than accurate targeting).[74] Just as well, since prepared dug-ins, mobility, fog and terrain mocked notions of easy take-out--witness the extraordinary low kill-ratios of the mass NATO sorties of August-September 1995 (see below).

Most death and damage was in fact caused by mortar shelling. All sides in Bosnia converted ambulances to allow mortars to be carried and fired, allowing firing 'protected' by civilian human shields, and near-instant mobility. These are **not** forces that are vulnerable to discriminate air attack.

Then there were the rape stories. Rape is integral to war and depravity; it is the rogue soldier's unholy price for death's threat. The less disciplined, more brutal and brutalized of all sides have surely sinned. But the mass rape charge, told by a Serb conscript in Muslim custody, and splashed and long-maintained on front pages and screens, was obviously preemptive; it denied attention to scrupulously documented non-governmental Serb investigations of rape and other atrocities against Serb women.[75] It also contained obvious and provable falsehoods, yet these were excised without mention by the *New York Times* and other media trend setters.[76]

Graphic images of Serb-perpetrated horrors were and are front page fodder, yet the horrendous images they counterpose--beheaded bodies floating down the Danube with signs

---

[74] Kai Brand-Jacobsen, *On the Ex-Yugoslav Quagmire; Interview with General Lewis Mackenzie*, 8 May 1993; available from ICWCB archives, Ottawa.

[75] When ICWCB officials first visited the Serbian Council Information Centre in Belgrade, the first former Yugoslav institution to attempt systematically to collate evidence on all war crimes allegations, including those directed against Serbs (which fact lost it all government funding), in February 1993, it had been visited by neither UN officials, nor *New York Times* or other journalists. See 'Rape and Sexual Abuse of Serb Women, Men and Children in Areas Controlled by Croatian and Moslem Formations in Bosnia and Herzegovina and Croatia, 1991-93', *Documentation on the Violation of Human Rights, Ethnic Cleansing and Violence by Croatian and Moslem Armed Formations Against the Serb Population in Bosnia-Herzegovina*, Belgrade: Serbian Council Information Centre, 1993; it presents incidence, rape trauma and other follow-up medical and psychological documentation on more than 7000 cases. See also 'Map of Settlements and Camps in Bosnia-Herzegovina and Croatia in which Systematic Rape and Sexual Harassment of Ethnic Serb Women, Men and Children was Performed', in the same compendium. The much larger number of Muslim victims subsequently alleged contrasts with a report from the Boston-based Physicians for Human Rights; their visits to Croatian and Bosnian hospitals found 119 women pregnant from asserted rape.

[76] The main such, that UN Commander Lewis Mackenzie had been engaged in his own mass rape rampage, was excised in initial and follow-up *New York Times* and other media reports, as rather too obviously influenced by Mackenzie's scrupulous reporting **also** of war crimes evidence against the Muslim government and its agents. No consideration was given to whether anti-Serb allegations might be similarly tainted.

47

saying 'to the meat-markets of Belgrade' and others, some witnessed by this author, are 'not fit to print'.[77] Indeed, **what** you see **does** affect you; and thus it matters where you go!

So also with stories of 'concentration camps'. Some individual outrage was sincere: American Jewish leader Eli Wiesel, taken to a camp by Serb hosts, shocked by the crowding, demanded and received the commandant's promise that all would be released; when the promise was rescinded, whether by higher, inter-mediate or local order, Wiesel issued a scathing indictment. Yet Croat and Muslim internment camps not visited by Wiesel were scarcely better, and he would later reconsider his apportioning of blame (after receiving US Holocaust Survivors documentation--some from Israeli archives and sources).[78] Other outrage was open to the charge of manipulation. *Time* magazine's camp victim coverage, for example, was blatantly skewered for anti-Serb effect.

Coverage of war crimes evidence and prosecution was analogous. The generally uncriticized UN-approved forms with which US, Canadian and other governments sought war crime witnesses were telling, and frightening. They required no corroboration. Like Nazi, Soviet and McCarthyite inducements to snitch, they encouraged the false, and thus blurred the true.

UN Ambassador Madeleine Albright and Canada's Colonel Fenrik (the UN's point man on war crimes) effectively acknowledged that the only accusations properly pursued, in Vukovar and elsewhere, were those against Serbs. Lack of money and other problems was said to preclude further-ranging effort. This is the Salem Witch Trials revisited; it mocks due process, and violates our most basic norms of ethics, morality and civilization.[79]

Preemptive and 'big lie' techniques featured prominently. Izetbegovic' story of massacre of Bijeljina's Muslims rallied support to his nascent state; the story retains pride of place in UN anthologies. Yet colleagues and I (scholars with no Serb blood, wives, or lovers) visited Bijeljina, spoke to local Muslims, with no Serb guides or ears, and recorded their testimony. Their story was different. They told of Mujaheddin mercenaries, sent to take the city and area (assuming support from co-religionists), to sever the Bosnian Serb heartland's lifeline to Serbia. Their approach was observed. The Yugoslav army was far away. Word went to Arkan's militia, across the Krajina border. Arkan's men intercepted and

---

[77] *Genocide Against the Serbs*, Belgrade: [private] Museum of Modern Art, 1992; 'Serbia's Truth and Paranoia--with caveats', in 'Yugoslavia's Wars of Succession', *op cit*; and ICWCB archives.

[78] Conversations with and documentation from John Ranz, Chairperson, Survivors of the Buchenwald Concentration Camp, February 1995; ICWCB archives.

[79] Not surprisingly, the politicized UN War Crimes prosecution efforts have shown no interest in ICWCB archives, or any other 'politically incorrect' (ie non-prejudiced) archive.

killed the mostly foreign force. Local Muslims were among those who appealed to Arkan, and guided him; they later raised a Muslim battalion to fight with Bosnian Serb forces on the northern front. This Civil War was always more complex than most outsiders realized. Arkan is not lily-white (he drew a pistol on me when he thought me a Croat spy, for I asked too many questions). But on this issue, the most arch-typal of UN 'cases', the evidence on the ground points elsewhere.

The media campaign, manipulated and gullible, continued. When President Clinton tentatively authorized bombing of Serb positions in May 1993, *Newsweek's* cover showed a Srebrenica boy wounded by Serb artillery, with no mention of the fact that the 150 UN trucks sent to evacuate him and others had been forced to leave empty; the local Muslim commander wanted human shields. The inside story began with three and a half pages of photographs of what could only be presumed to be victims of Serbs, yet the locales noted in their captions identified them, obscurely and late in the text that followed, as victims of Muslim-Croat fighting. *Time's* cover claimed to show a Serb shooting a wounded man in Brcko. Yet the incendiary picture was in fact taken by *Reuters* a year earlier (as acknowledged at the bottom left of the table of content page), in Slovenia, not Brcko. The soldier was not Serb, and his pointed gun was not shooting.

The *New York Times'* Pulitzer Prize winning Bosnia correspondent talked of Bosnia's 1000 years of inter-ethnic and religious peace, betraying a historical ignorance so profound as to make flat earth believers look omniscient. But then the *Times* was and is wondrously consistent: it rightly blames Serbs when the evidence so warrants; it also blames Serbs when UN ground commanders find reason to believe Serb accusations that Jihad (Holy War) fanatics have perpetrated massacres on their own to 'prove' Serb perfidy.[80]

And this kind of 'reporting', was and is no aberration. Again and again the *New York Times*, the *Washington Post*, France's *L'Express* and *L'Observateur* and other Western media leaders offered photographs of armed men carrying visible Ustasha and Muslim identification, with captions identifying them as Serb. Pictures of Vukovar devastation were captioned Dubrovnik (pictures of an apparently resurrected Dubrovnik, with significant damage only to Serb heritage, were not 'fit to print').

Stories of Serb 'cleansing' were plentiful, with no mention of the now-disappeared one third of Mostar's pre-war population who identified themselves as Serbs or Yugoslavs, or of Srebrenica's pre-war Serb population, or other cities'. Nor of the irony that the single most sweeping ethnic cleansing of the Bosnian wars prior to 1995's massive expulsions of

---

[80] See ie report in *The Times* (of London), 19 February 1994; also *Truth is the Victim in Bosnia*, Truth in Journalism Project, The (Jewish) Anti-Defamation League, New York, June 1993.

Serbs was of Muslims by Muslims: the 5th Corp's Fall 1994 offensive against dissident Muslims in Bihac made at least 55,000 homeless.

Horror at the Serb offensive in Eastern Bosnia in April 1993; no mention of the Muslim offensive that first swept the region in April 1992. Horror at the Serb offensive against Bihac in late 1994, and the Serb shelling of Tuzla and other 'safe havens' in March 1995; no mitigating coverage of the fact that each responded to Muslim government offensives that thrust out from these 'havens', contravening previously brokered truce agreements. The US-dominated Security Council decision to ignore peacekeeper warnings that 'safe havens' would mean Muslim military havens if **all** assault was not banned, remained a media non-topic.

Horror that Serbs expected to retain a larger proportion of land than warranted by their percentage of the population; no mention of the fact that they had owned a similar proportion before the war (see above) or that this larger proportion was the least endowed in industry, power and other resources. Lands are not synonymous; an acre of Saharan sand does not equal an acre of Manhattan real estate.

Support for 'self determination' for Croats and Muslims, but not for Serbs. Serb aspirations for a united nation, once approved by Presidents Woodrow Wilson and Roosevelt (with far more generous territorial swath than the Serbs' maximum 'spoils of war'), were labelled Greater Serbia, an obscenity; Greater Croatia, however, even extended to incorporate ancestral Serb lands, was and is seen as a natural right; so is Greater Muslim Bosnia, extended to incorporate both Serb and Croat lands (though Presidents Wilson and Roosevelt, like Nazi Germany, acknowledged Bosnia as historical Serb heartland).

1995: Washington's/NATO's war; uncertain peace

The unleashed fury of NATO air power against the Bosnian Serbs in August-September 1995 and the uncertain (dictated?) peace that followed appeared, to some, as the logical culmination of a dominant long term Western war approach policy. Yet the course of events obfuscated as much as it clarified. NATO's aggressive posture had multiple roots.

One reflected the proclaimed, accumulating 'humiliation' of past restraint-**cum**-'appeasement' in response to Serb resolve-**cum**-'intransigence'; the politically correct asserted dire threat to NATO's credibility and future. A second root grew from Slobodan Milosevic' 1994 embrace of minimalist aims (reflected in his acceptance of the five-power Contact Group formula assigning 49 per cent of Bosnia to Bosnian Serb authority, the remaining 51 per cent to the US-mediated Muslim-Croat 'federation'), his consequent split with Krajina and Srbska leaders, now described as self-serving, corrupt and worse (justifying the imposition of a near total embargo on non-humanitarian Serb aid) and his break with Vojislav Seselj, the fiery nationalist leader, who was also reviled--and later imprisoned for leading a banned demonstration. Milosevic' withdrawal from the ethno-religious national agenda has been variously ascribed, as responding to war, sanctions and deprivation wariness (an easing of sanctions was secured), as constituency re-shaping responding to and conceding others' greater nationalist appeal, and/or as confirmation of a strategic deal with Croatia that would ultimately partition Bosnia between the larger states.[81]

Covert German, US and allied military aid, through 'deniable' procurement channels funnelling former GDR fighter aircraft to Zagreb and other heavy equipment to both Croatia and Muslim Bosnia, and the provision of 'retired' military and intelligence training personnel, is documentable as early as 1991. But the months following former President Carter's successful December 1994 cease-fire negotiations saw a marked increase in deliveries, notably through US-manned Hercules transports to Tuzla and other airfields, and jumbo jet deliveries from Iran.[82] Croatia's lightning conquest of 'UN-protected' Western Slavonia in May 1995, which expelled more than 85,000 Serbs, was a direct outgrowth of this aid--and Belgrade's (agreed?) refusal to intervene.

The Bosnian Muslim government's subsequent rejection of the Carter truce and announced intent to break the siege of Sarajevo fared less well: initial successes were followed by devastating defeat. Buoyed by their success around Sarajevo, perceiving licence in the international acceptance of Western Slavonia's fate, and perhaps responding to anticipated Croatian action against Krajina, the Bosnian Serb army then overran the 'protected' Muslim enclaves of Zepa and Srebrenica in Eastern Bosnia in July.

Croatia's **blitzkrieg** offensive against Krajina in August mocked Knin leader Milan Babic' acceptance of Zagreb's Z4 plan at the United Nations' Geneva headquarters the day before (and thus also the 'Contact Group', since the plan essentially implemented its formula for reintegration in return for local autonomy guarantees). Its sweeping success--following

---

[81] On early Tudjman-Milosevic discussions, direct and indirect, see Zeljko Vukovic, 'Da li su Tudjman i Milosevic delili BiH', *Vreme*, 10 June 1991; *The Times* (London), 12 July 1991; and *Novi Vjesnik* (Zagreb), 8 May 1992.

[82] The Tuzla deliveries (up to four a day) followed the 1994 agreement with Karadzic to allow 'humanitarian flights', to be verified as such by Russian UN inspectors on the ground; the inspections proviso was circumvented; in fact no shipment inspection was allowed; radio intercepts and other evidence confirms military deliveries. For further information See ie T.B. Carr, 'German and US Involvement in the Balkans: A Careful Coincidence of National Policies?', and Sean Gervasi, 'Bosnia and Vietnam: Another Quagmire', presented to *Symposium on the Balkan War. Yugoslavia: Past and Present* (to be publ.), Chicago, 31 August -1 September 1995; also 'US allows Iran to arm Muslims in Bosnia', *Montreal Gazette* (from *Washington Post*), 15 April 1995.

51

Belgrade's refusal to intervene, the not unrelated Bosnian Serb army's refusal to heed Radovan Karadzic' contrary call, and consequent orders to Krajina Serb units to withdraw rather than fight--also restored Muslim Bosnian morale and ambition. The Sarajevo government reiterated its commitment to a 'military solution'.

In this they were clearly encouraged by the persistent, quintessential 'war approach' partisanship of Western commentary: having ignored the Croat and Muslim leaderships' initial embrace of ethno-religious exclusivity, it now continued to downplay or dismiss Croat or Muslim culpability even as these leaderships enacted ethno-religious policies that ever-more starkly contradicted their rhetoric.[83] Cease and desist demands were directed at Serbs alone, not the Muslim army or its Mojaheddin mercenaries. With a quarter million Serbs cleansed from Krajina amidst killings of civilians and refugees (documented by UN and other sources and, in some cases, CNN cameras), the *New York Times* and Madeleine Albright focused instead, uncritically, on a contested Muslim charge of Serb terror in Srebrenica. The pattern, long set, would be repeated.

Bosnia's Serb leadership was clearly divided (Karadzic had to rescind his dismissal of army chief Radko Mladic in the face of army and other opposition), though not on bottom-line negotiating criteria. Karadzic had previously accepted the 51-49 per cent formula, with obvious reluctance. But he had adamantly rejected the first implementing map draft, which skewered the land split into a 80-20 resources division in favour of the Sarajevo government, and on this issue there was no disunity. When more equitable subsequent drafts (due largely to British and French intervention) conceded the point, as well as the necessity of self-governing authority for the divided entities, Karadzic announced his acceptance.[84]

The timing of the Sarajevo shell or bomb that provided official justification for NATO's air war was thus peculiar, the more so as it came just days after formal transfer of operational bombing authority from the UN Secretary General's office to NATO--whose spokesmen promised robust and disproportionate response to Serb provocation.[85] [And,

[83] See ie Francis Wheen, 'Say What? Making small talk with Tudjman', *Ottawa Citizen* (from the *Guardian*), 3 May 1995; Julian Borger, 'Croatia shuts out ethnic minorities', *Guardian Weekly*, 27 August 1995; Remy Ourdan, 'The Bosnian dream of a multi-ethnic future is dying', *Guardian Weekly* (from *Le Monde*), 9 October 1994; and 'Bosnia The coffee-cup state', *The Economist*, 26 August 1995.

[84] See ie Ronald Hatchett, 'Don't ignore the Serbs' peace plan', *Dallas Morning News*, 4 August 1995, and his 'The Search for a Negotiated Solution to the Balkan Crisis' presentation to the August 31-September 1 Symposium, *op cit*.

[85] Ian Traynor, 'Nato takes charge of air strike policy', *The Guardian Weekly*, 27 August 1995.

indeed, the assignation of blame was later refuted by senior UN officers on the ground as well as off-the-record US Administration and Pentagon officials.][86]

The unfolding of the air war, which struck military, infrastructure and unintended civilian targets throughout Srbska, was also peculiar. Karadzic decried the blame and response, but accepted the demanded lifting of the siege of Sarajevo and the withdrawal of Serb heavy weapons. But Mladic refused to comply, insisting that withdrawal without assurances of Muslim restraint would doom then-exposed Serb communities. His refusal became justification for the continuation and escalation of NATO attacks, which culminated in cruise missile strikes against the Banja Luka area and near exhausted 'military target' lists.

Against the backdrop of vociferous Russian protest and internal NATO opposition to escalation to what would be all-out war, the previously refused assurances demanded by Mladic were now given--through UN and other intermediaries.[87] With Serb withdrawals proceeding under media and UN inspectors' glare, air strike critics were largely vindicated; perhaps 90 per cent of Serb artillery, tanks and heavy weapons had in fact survived the bombing waves, though the destruction of transport (especially bridges) and communication nodes would clearly constrict Serb mobility and potential in other areas.

And it was to some of these areas that attention now shifted, as a combined Croat-Muslim offensive swept through southwestern Bosnia, breaking the Serb and rebel Muslim siege of Bihac, and ultimately threatening Banja Luka, the heartland of western Srbska. But, again, the course of events was peculiar. Mladic departed from Sarajevo, not to the new battle field, but to a kidney operation in Belgrade. The Bosnian Serb retreat occasioned huge refugee numbers (perhaps 100,000 reached Banja Luka, further compounding the Krajina refugee crisis), yet Srbska military units apparently retreated in orderly manner--they were not overrun.[88]

---

[86] David Binder, 'Nato Misfire? Bosnia's Bombers', *The Nation*, 2 October 1995; Binder furthermore notes that Canadian officers in Sarajevo were now convinced that Muslim government forces detonated **both** the 5 February 1994 and the 28 August market massacres blamed on Serb forces. See also Hugh McManners (Defence Correspondence), 'Serbs 'not guilty' of massacre--Experts warned US that mortar was Bosnian', *Sunday Times*, London, 1 October 1995; and George Kenney, 'US troops in Bosnia couldn't be impartial', *The Washington Times*, 11 October 1995.

[87] See ie Aileen McCabe, 'Serb president agrees to lift Sarajevo siege', *Ottawa Citizen*, 15 September 1995; also *New York Times* coverage, 15 and 16 September 1995.

[88] The Serbian army leadership in fact anticipated the attack route of the Croat-Muslim offensive, and was confident of the defenders' ability to hold--if so ordered; see ie 'Kako Odbraniti Krajinu', *Duga*, Belgrade, 9 June 1995.

As the Croat-Muslim offensive proceeded to effect a *de facto* 50-50 division of Bosnia, approximating the contact group charter, there were reports of reinforced and no longer yielding Serb defences around Banja Luka, and Western calls for negotiations. The Croatian army announced its disengagement. The Sarajevo government, however, encouraged by further commitments of money, arms and men from Muslim countries, from Iran to Malaysia, refused to abandon the war option, threatened the Sarajevo resolution with mortar strikes against the Serb suburb, and, when repulsed south of Banja Luka, launched new attacks against the 'corridor' connecting western and eastern Srbska--seeking moral sanction through the announced discovery of a grave site allegedly containing bones of Muslim or Croat dead.

Sarajevo reiterated its insistence on a unified Bosnia, with its corollary of Serb defeat. But stiffened Serb defences in this region also, and more forceful British, US and other calls for restraint, brought the Muslim government to the negotiating table. On 26 September all sides signed the confirming agreement to ratify the creation of two self-governing 'entities' under the *pro forma* aegis of a tripartite central presidency, though exact demarcation borders and other implementing details remained disputed and/or unclear; still simmering fighting underlined the agreement's fragility.

Ironically, the 'two entities' formula was essentially a return to the pre-war agreement negotiated by Britain's Lord Carrington, but then repudiated by Izetbegovic, with war the foreseeable and inevitable consequence. One might note that a similar formula, if imposed on Croatia, would likely have averted war there also. Ethnic groups fundamentally alienated from each other by differing interpretations of history, faith and culture, and especially minorities fearing survival, must be given the security respite of distinct space under their own or neutral authority or guarantee. To refuse such security is to acquiesce in the consequences--which in Croatia's case brought the alternative, stark solution of the largest ethnic cleansing of modern times.

The agreement may prove a turning point in Bosnia if fleshed out by substance--or but a respite, for there are others' agendas on all sides that decree rejection. And the larger context of ex-Yugoslavia still posits dangerous conundrums, not least the final Eastern Slavonia sliver of Krajina (whose population has swelled with Western Slavonia refugees) neighbouring Serbia proper, and Kosovo. But the pattern of 1994-95 events, both those that did happen and those that did not, clearly suggests a parallel-tracking of the principle players' personal and political agendas, and at least a roughly agreed design for resolution.

And if this is true, then NATO's bombing war must be seen in disturbing new light. If its purported purpose and rationale was incidental, then why was it launched? Was it deemed necessary to forestall the threatened larger-scale intervention by Muslim states, whether coordinated or competitive (and thus doubly escalatory), which in turn posited the spectre of all-out Serb/Yugoslav involvement, Greek and Bulgar intervention, and perhaps that of others? Or (assuming Muslim interventions could be deterred through other means, as appears likely) was it motivated primarily by NATO and leadership PR considerations and the need to release the pent-up furies of 'Punish Serbs' theologians--furies that in some cases had intensified in perverse reverse proportion to accumulating evidence that black-white blame designations were simplistic, to say the least--? Disturbing thoughts indeed.

*

War Crimes; what CAN be done? Yes, let us have a War Crimes Tribunal, though a War Crimes Tribunal focused on ex-Yugoslav lands must at least in principle be a precursor for one with global mandate and responsibility. Laws that don't apply to all are a mockery of justice. So also with regard to the entities that seceded from and succeeded former Yugoslavia. Serb allegations and evidence must be investigated with the same resources accorded Croat and Muslim claims. **All** rape cases must be followed up, as they would be in Washington, London or Paris, with gynaecological and other evidence (including follow-up psychiatric and rape case worker reports) sought and verified.

The Vukovar grave site of presumed Croat victims of Serb massacre must be exhumed, **as must the many more Vukovar sites where Serbs allege earlier Croat massacre**. Similar crimes must be accorded similar rules of evidence, similar standards of proof. Crimes must be generic, not defined by ethnicity or faith. To prosecute Karadzic and Mladic while exculpating Tudjman and Izetbegovic, whose followers committed equal or worse and earlier atrocities, mocks elementary notions of justice. To allow *a priori* partisan assertions of guilt to dictate and limit investigatory follow-up, as championed by Madeleine Albright and Colonel Fenrik, the war crimes evidence coordinator, is to prescribe a Kangaroo court no better than Salem's.[89] We can and must do better--or cease what will otherwise be seen as judicial farce.

*

Resolution--? As for the war's resolution, the alternatives are stark. One is to embed the limited-purpose military persuasion and the complementary **and ultimately conditional** nonpartisan rebuilding and developmental commitments that underlay the September 1995

---

[89] The War Crimes Tribunal's readiness to issue post-arrest indictments against previously non-indicted Serb officers (as happened after Muslim forces arrested/kidnapped General Djukic and Colonel Krsmanovic on January 30th 1996) compounded the insult to justice, and to norms of procedure.

agreements, and that remain crucial to its implementation and prospects. The Ohio accord signed on November 21 appeared to do just that, though implementation prospects remained threatened and befogged.[90]

The second, if this fails, is to give the field back to the combatants, until they exhaust themselves. If accompanied by strictures against outside involvement, this would probably doom Bosnian Muslim space to ultimate division between successor Croat and Serb states.

The third is UN withdrawal accompanied by formal lifting of the arms embargo and non-enforced strictures against outside involvement. This would likely lead to significantly increased overt deliveries of Islamic government and perhaps US arms to the Izetbegovic government and an inevitably escalating infusion of both Turkish and harder-Islamic contingents; it would also compel much larger scale Serb and Croat intervention (and likely cooperation) and, probably, Greek and Bulgarian support to Serbia--the same spectre that NATO's 1995 air war may have been designed to avert. Another Balkan War.

The fourth solution, a Washington/UN imposed partisan *diktat*, with unlimited military force and not accompanied by the carrot of postwar development prospects for all, could require far larger troop numbers than envisioned by most analysts. World War 2 German and allied troop numbers, though not of uniform quality, ultimately totalled about 500,000--in a losing cause.

The first choice, essentially a re-embrace of the old Carrington formula as well as a reflection of international law's latest 'Quebec posture' is clearly preferable. Its extension to Serb Krajina (recognizing that region's secessionist referendum) has been made moot by force of condoned arms and 'cleansing'. But a variant involving autonomy if not independence, as called for in the Contact Group/Z4 Krajina finesse, might yet resolve the status of now more heavily Serb populated and Yugoslav/Serb army protected Eastern

---

[90] See ie John Pomfret's report in *The Washington Post*, 22 November 1995; one problem: Milan Milanovic, head of the Serb negotiating team, was emphatic that the Tudjman-Milosevic deal on Eastern Slavonia (see text below) "does not prejudice the final political solution"; another is suggested by Momcilo Krajisnik, President of the Srbska Parliament, who noted that the deal was signed behind the back of the Bosnian Serb delegation, and objected to a number of its provisions, especially that which assigned Sarajevo's Serb suburbs to Muslim control, *Internet*, 21 November--though Bosnian Serbs were pleased that Russian peacekeepers would patrol the crucial Posavina/Brcko corridor, their lifeline to Serbia.

A potentially graver problem, and potential deal-breaker (intra-NATO as well as on the ground), emerged subsequently, with US acquiescence in the Izetbegovic government's refusal to expel Iranian military/terror instructors and Mujaheddin, as stipulated in the Dayton accords--they were instead protected by 'diplomatic immunity' or granted Muslim Bosnian citizenship; see ie John Pomfret, 'US Trains Troops With Links to Iran', *The Guardian Weekly*, 4 February 1996; Philip Smucker, 'Europeans oppose arming of Muslims', *The Toronto Globe and Mail*, 15 March 1996; or C.G. Jacobsen, 'Washington's Balkan Strategy: Aberration or Herald?', *The South Slav Journal* (London), March 1966.

Slavonia. Milosevic and Tudjman in fact signed a deal to this effect during the Ohio negotiations. Memories of August cautioned against optimism, though Milosevic commanded resources that Babic had not.

There are no easy choices, and no choices without cost. The first compelling requirement, however, is thorough, unblinkered reevaluation, of what has happened, and what may yet happen. The tentative agreement of September, codified in November 1995, proffered hope that this process had finally begun, but it is a beginning still fraught with question.

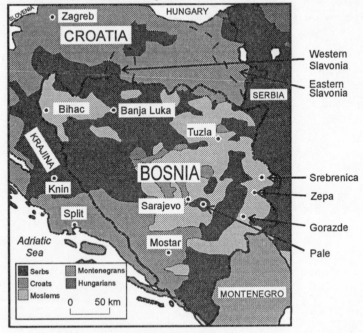

Nations and Nationalities According to the 1981 Census
Croatia, Bosnia, Montenegro and Western Serbia

Bosnia Divided; the Dayton Agreement

5 Eurasia's 'Times of Trouble'

ABSTRACT: Russia's military has been both victim and agent of the revolutionary changes that have swept the lands of Muscovy since 1988. Though wreaked by dynamics that defied control, it has emerged as perhaps the most important arbiter of (still uncertain) societal cohesion and purpose. To appreciate the complex interplay of often contradictory nationalist, ethnic-separatist, socioeconomic and other dynamics that shaped the years from withdrawal from empire to Boris Yeltsin's (second) coup in September 1993 and beyond, the topic must perforce be subdivided into period and thematic subsections. The analysis looks first at the forces and events that led to the failed coup of August 1991, and Yeltsin's successful usurpation of power shortly thereafter. This is followed by a thematic overview of the economic dynamics (budgetary collapse, conversion and arms trade imperatives) that span these and later events. The analysis then turns to the milestones that shaped the 1993 emergence of a new, far smaller, but again ambitious Great Russian Army--once again accepted as Russia's revolutionary arbiter, but now free of the social compact that had bound it through previous eras of Russian history. The final section looks at Yeltsin's inglorious Chechnya campaign, the Army's remarkable 'stand-down' from the campaign and the startling consequences of that stand-down.

Arms and Society; Russia's revolutionary arbiter

Military transformation as weather-vane for the turmoil that swept through and changed the lands of Rus from 1988 to 1993 is uniquely appropriate. Since Peter the Great, under tsars and commissars, the army was integrated into a larger, composite leadership. Its officers served on the highest councils of state, and party. It participated in policy formulation, and frequently also implementation, in economic, social and other realms. Its stewardship of the

59

Orthodox Church under Peter, its 'school of the nation' role and purpose, and the fact that it was called on to provide leadership for Mikhail Gorbachev's attempt to generate civilian high technology industries, are symptomatic. Conversely, civilian state and party leaders served on military councils, affecting, and in turn being affected by, military decision-making, concerns and ethos.[91]

In other words, the army was always part of and never apart from the nation's leadership; the concept of military coup or regime was alien to its culture and tradition. Russian history resounds to the memory of peasant rebellions against the established order, to names like Stenka Razin and Emelian Pugachev. Yet the army, as an institution, always remained loyal. There were mutinies, notably the 1825 Decembrist (Guards) revolt against the accession of Nicholas 1; the Petrograd garrison's defection in 1917; and the Kronstadt (Fleet) revolt of 1921, which, as Lenin said, 'lit up reality better than anything else', and led to Lenin's New Economic Policy. Yet the changes they wrought reflected the larger dynamics of which they were part, not the nature of their métier--they were societal agents, not military.

Nevertheless, history reminds us that notions of role and duty are not always synonymous with *status quo*; they may also serve forces of societal change. The army as a whole has never truly led such forces of change. But in the past it has signalled the death of the old order, as when Marshal Alexsey Brusilov and many of the Tsar's finest officers 'stood down' in 1917, and it has been decisive in defining the new, as when these officers rallied to the Red Army after the Polish invasion in 1920.[92]

In August 1991, also, the army effectively 'stood down', thwarting the coup plotters' attempt to revive the old order. The voices of Russian President Boris Yeltsin at the Russian parliament, Vice President Alexander Rutskoi on Moscow's *Ekho* radio, and Mayor Anatoly Sobchak in Leningrad signalled societal change. But it was the physical intervention of some of the armed forces' premier units that protected, and thus confirmed, change.

By summer 1992, and even more pronouncedly in September 1993, when Yeltsin suspended legislature and constitution and declared personal rule, the army had also become instrumental in defining the evolution and nature of that change. To understand the winds of change, the crucible of revolution, and the nature of the new, emerging order, however, one must first go back to 1988.

---

[91] See for example C.G. Jacobsen (ed.), *Strategic Power: USA/USSR*, London/New York: Macmillan and St. Martin's Press, 1990, chapters 3, 7, 27, 31, 38, 42 and 43.

[92] A. Levitskii, 'General Brusilov', *Voennaya byl* (January 1968), p 19; see also David R. Jones, 'The Youth of General A.A. Brusilov: the making of the unconventional, conventional professional', address to The Royal Military College, Kingston, March 1992 (and available from same).

From Revolution Controlled to Revolution Unleashed

Elected General Secretary in 1985, Mikhail Gorbachev hoisted the banner of Revolution Controlled. His election signalled acceptance of the thesis first put forward by Mikhail Suslov, the Party's old ideologue, in 1977, that there was now dangerous contradiction between a fossilised party-rule superstructure and a much better educated, more sophisticated population base; the former must be reformed, to reflect the demands and aspirations of the latter. Gorbachev embraced Nikita Khrushchev's failed slogans of 'Return of Socialist Legality...and Leninist Norms', and re-packaged them in calls for *Glasnost* [openness] and *Perestroika* [rebuilding]. His goal was that of Czechoslovakia's Alexander Dubcek, crushed by Soviet tanks in 1968: communism with a human face--or social democracy.[93]

The socioeconomic attempt to rebuild was four-pronged.[94] There were campaigns against corruption and alcoholism (the initial focus also of former General Secretary Yuri Andropov's reform agenda, before his untimely death in 1983). There was a significant freeing of central controls and increased acceptance of independent entrepreneurship, at least in the services and small business sectors. Administrative and production facilities seen to be inefficient were reorganized--though, as with Khrushchev's similar efforts, the new constructs often addressed symptoms rather than the disease, and usually had little effect. Finally, resources were funnelled to 'industries of the future', in a conscious and military-supported attempt to build a civilian high technology industry to complement and interact synergistically with the hard-pressed advanced branches of military industry.

Military support for this effort, for Gorbachev's across the board arms control and reductions campaign to end the confrontational nature of East–West relations and secure Western trade, aid and investment opportunities, and for withdrawal from foreign involvements--in Afghanistan, Mongolia and Eastern Europe--derived from two doctrinal revolutions.

The first, confirmed by Leonid Brezhnev's Tula speech and the emergence of Marshal Nikolai Ogarkov as Chief of the General Staff in 1977, relegated nuclear arms to the role of ultimate deterrent, and focused future efforts on the combined operations potentials of new conventional and other more revolutionary technologies (laser, high energy particle beam, and so on) that promised nuclear effect, but with far more precision and far

---

[93] When asked the difference between Gorbachev's spring in 1987 and Dubcek's in 1968, Soviet spokesman Gennadi Gerasimov's answer was to the point: '19 years!'; see Charles Gati, 'Gorbachev and Eastern Europe', *Foreign Affairs*, Summer 1987, p 972.

[94] Jacobsen (ed.), *Strategic Power*, chapters 7, 27 and 42.

less collateral damage. Nuclear threat spectres were in effect said to have been checkmated; the focus was switched to other threats that might be relevant in the 21st century. Ironically, the Gulf War in early 1991, with its 'smart' weaponry, which some saw as victory over Soviet arms, was victory only over largely obsolescent Soviet arms, and, in fact, validation of Ogarkov's charter for the future.

The second doctrinal revolution, more intimately associated with Gorbachev's name, was that calling for only 'sufficient defence', 'defensive defence', and acceptance of 'mutual security'; the old zero-sum view that insecurity for one meant security for the other was now seen as dangerous delusion--prescription for arms race and war. The doctrine first emerged indirectly, in an article (coauthored by Andrey Kokoshin, Moscow's foremost civilian strategist) reevaluating the Battle of Kursk, the largest tank battle of the Second World War. It gave artillery barrages the primary credit for victory--though *tankisti* were credited for the pace and extent of later German withdrawals.

The article was seminal. It struck at the core thesis of Soviet nuclear and non-nuclear doctrine since the war: that good defence rests on readiness to preempt offensively. The doctrine now developed owed its intellectual roots to Western conflict theorists shunned by their own governments, notably Anatol Rappoport, to the Stockholm International Peace Research Institute and the Report of the Palme Commission (chaired by former Swedish Prime Minister Oluf Palme). It was also a logical extension of Ogarkov's doctrine. To his premise of nuclear stalemate and new, high technology future needs--an expensive recipe, as the latter costs far more than the former--it brought particular attention to the theoretically unlimited range of new defence technologies, and a dimension of time luxury that was absent from Ogarkov.

The changes were crucial. Ogarkov may have identified the technological requirements of future wars, but the continuing immediacy of his threat spectrum allowed no question of Moscow's oldest dogma--that maximum in-place force must be deployed along the periphery of empire. This was dictated by the constraint of abysmal communication and transportation infrastructures, vitiating prospects for reinforcement. In the context of 1000–year ethnocentric memories of periphery war, this always translated into larger armed forces' structures than might otherwise have been necessary. Thus also in Eastern Europe: 'bought with the blood of 20 million' (now revised upwards to 27.7 million), the perceived need for hegemony echoed the names of Hitler, the Kaiser, Napoleon, and Charles, and the fact that east of the Tatras, the land runs flat to Moscow; the visceral nature of the demand was reflected also in the fact that the 'Iron Curtain' was a near replica of a line first drawn on the map by Catherine the Great, as the line east of which Moscow could afford no hostile dominion.

The new doctrine negated the premise that underlay periphery force deployments, in Tsarist and Soviet days, and that made maximum buffer extensions a strategic necessity, whatever the cost. It established the military rationale for withdrawals, and for substantive reductions not only in the nuclear arsenal, but also, and more importantly, in conventional force numbers--by far the costliest part of the defence establishment. Thus it also provided *ipso facto* leeway for continued funding of high technology aspirations even in the context of significantly declining overall defence budgets.

*

Withdrawal and contraction: change unleashed. Gorbachev's December 1988 UN Speech announcing unilateral Soviet Army manpower cuts of 500,000 was followed in 1989 by withdrawal from Afghanistan, the announcement that the Soviet defence budget would be cut by 14 per cent, and withdrawal of Soviet support for East European client regimes--their death knell. Negotiations on total troop withdrawal schedules were begun that year with Germany, Poland, Czechoslovakia, Hungary and Mongolia.

The scale and pace of subsequent withdrawal rates was wrenching; the revolution wrought imposed its own dynamic and momentum--its impact was, in fact, eerily reminiscent of that of the Petrograd Soviet's Order Number One of 14 March 1917. The Soviet contingent in Afghanistan, withdrawn by February 1989, totalled about 115,000. The 73,500 troops in Czechoslovakia and 65,000 in Hungary, plus 50,000 from Mongolia, and some of the 50,000 in Poland and 350,000 in Germany, were out by 1991. The withdrawal from Poland was completed in 1992 (except for 2000, to facilitate troop transports from Germany), that from Germany in 1994.

The return of nearly 700,000 (army and air force, with weapons, logistics and all base removables), most of whom could not be absorbed by a now contracting force structure, was wrenching for morale and discipline.[95] German finance would pay for 36,000 homes, but most returnees were condemned to grossly inadequate and crowded housing, or tent cities. There were already 175,000 military families without proper living conditions before the

---

[95] The scale of the effort is indicated by the following: 73,500 troops, 1220 tanks, 2505 heavy vehicles, 1218 artillery pieces, 77 planes and 146 attack helicopters from Hungary (Vladimir Skutina, *Rusove' Prichazeji a Odchazeji* (Prague 1990)); 49,700 troops (originally 65,000), 50,000 dependents, 27,146 combat vehicles (including 860 tanks, 600 self-propelled artillery pieces and 1500 armoured infantry vehicles), and 560,000 tons of materiel (including 230,000 tons of ammunition and fuel) from Hungary (Zoltan Barany, 'A Hungarian Dream Comes True', *Report on Eastern Europe*, 7 March 1990); withdrawals from Germany alone would require 12,850 trains, each composed of 80 cars (*Report on Eastern Europe*, 10 May 1991).

withdrawals from Czechoslovakia and Hungary began; with these withdrawals and others, from Poland and Germany, the number swelled to 275,000.[96]

And housing was not the only problem. As many as a quarter of a million children also returned, to already bursting class sizes. The returnees also exacerbated the separatist and inter-ethnic dynamics unleashed by withdrawal from empire and the concomitant introduction of more democratic structures and procedures. Thus many settled in the Baltic Republics, and Kaliningrad--some because their roots were there; others because of better housing and quality of life prospects. The influx of Russian military retirees added fuel to the forces of exclusive nationalism and separatism. These, again, inflamed Russian nationalism, and Russians' very different concepts of historical rights.[97]

Glasnost filled in the 'white spots' of Stalinist and later history, from Red Army atrocities when reabsorbing the Baltic states after the Nazi–Soviet pact of 1939, to more recent brutalities of hazing and racial discrimination and worse (one report attributed all or most of 6–10,000 military deaths from 'suspicious circumstances' between 1985 and 1990 to this *dedovshchina*). In the new context of political tolerance, dissidence was nurtured and spread. Conscription intakes fell, as separatists in the Baltics, Georgia and elsewhere openly urged defiance.[98]

Local crackdown attempts, in Tbilisi in April 1989 and Baku in January 1990, served only to inflame local passions. The deaths of Tbilisi became the banner that brought V. Gamsakhurdia to the presidency--where the former dissident and Shakespeare scholar transformed himself into dictator and racist; when driven from office, though, he acknowledged no irony in effectively allying himself with the very minorities whose rights he had suppressed. His chameleon-like proclivities, and cavalier attitudes towards civil rights, proved not unrepresentative of the emerging class of 'democratic' politicians, especially those now emerging in the former Baltic republics (see below).

Tbilisi was also symptomatic of the counter-trend. The commander in charge of the crackdown, Colonel-General Igor Rodionov, an Afghan war veteran, vilified by democrats, was lionised by advocates of reimposed discipline--by force if and when necessary. The former, led by reserve officer Vladimir Lopatin, secured significant representation in the first

---

[96] *Report on Eastern Europe*, 7 September 1990.

[97] C.G. Jacobsen, 'Inviolable Borders: prescription for peace--or war?' *European Security*, Spring 1992.

[98] *Izvestia*, 22 July 1991, reported a near ten per cent short-fall, not counting 200,000 (annual) student deferments. See also 'Student deferments and Military Manpower Shortages', *Report on the USSR*, 2 August 1991.

elected Supreme Soviet, or parliament, but so did those riding the backlash against anarchy and dissolution, notably Colonels Alksnis and Petrushenko, the 'Black Colonels'. The latter achieved notoriety for a November 1990 ultimatum to Gorbachev, demanding his resignation if his reforms could not be made to work within 30 days. The two demanded a 'Committee of National Salvation'.[99]

Reaction against separatism also spawned the reestablishment of Cossack paramilitary formations, purportedly independent, but with clear ties to Russian nationalist forces, within and without the military, and three new Ministry of the Interior special forces type internal security formations.[100] The premier of these was the *Omon*. The initial organisation of *Omon*, in particular, appears to have been somewhat haphazard. Its emergence represented the confluence of two phenomena: now unemployed ex-army paratroop and special forces officers and soldiers unable to integrate into the civilian economy and seeking a new role for which their expertise might still be relevant, and Moscow's increasing concern as to the ramifications of lost social control. But, with regard to the crackdowns of December 1990-January 1991, there remains uncertainty as to whether the dog wagged the tail, or vice versa.

The culmination of the crackdowns, in Vilnius, Lithuania, in January 1991 (nine people died), is variously ascribed. The newly emerged independent military union *Shchit* [Shield], claimed that Colonel-General Vladislav Achalov, former Commander of the Airborne Assault Forces and then Deputy Minister of Defence, was the 'officer in charge', and that 'the President must have known about the planned action'.[101] A highly respected Western specialist arrived at a different conclusion: he saw the Vilnius *Omon* detachment at the time as, in effect, a *Freikorps*, composed of Russian ex-paratroopers from the region; he noted that the Landsbergis government had recently permitted former Lithuanian Nazi divisions to enact reunions in the capital; to chauvinist Russians, who remembered also Landsbergis' father's welcome to German troops in 1941, this was provocation beyond endurance.[102]

---

[99] Sovinform hypermedia on-disk release *Soviet Military Series #1; 1989–91: Transformation & Transition*, Carleton University Soviet National Security ORU, 1991.

[100] The OPNAZ motor rifle divisions (74,000 men in 1990); the SPETSNAZ (about 2500); and OMON (8000 as of May 1991)--see *Report on the USSR*, 31 May 1991.

[101] *Moscow News*, 3-19 March 1991.

[102] David R. Jones, Director of the Russian Institute of Nova Scotia and the Russian Microproject (and editor of the *Soviet Armed Forces Review Annual[s]* and *The Encyclopedia of Russian and Soviet Military History and Affairs)*, presentation to Carleton University's Institute of Soviet and East European Studies, March

In any case, in December 1990 Colonel-General Boris Gromov, Hero of the Soviet Union (and of Moscow's withdrawal from Kabul) and Commander of the Kiev Military District, accepted appointment as Deputy Minister of the Interior, with the mandate to rein in and/or organize/re-organize existing *Omon* and like units, and expand these into a national network of special forces security troops. He resigned his commission in January 1991 to take up his new duties, apparently foregoing army leadership prospects and a Marshal's star for a policeman's job--the last wish of any soldier. When asked why, he answered simply: 'fear of the Afghanisation of Soviet society'; what did he mean?: 'Grazhdanskaya Voina' [Civil War!].[103] It was a measure of profound concern.

*

Military reform, democracy and reaction: the attempted coup. The armed forces, as also the KGB--and as any army or security organisation would be--were cautious of those who advocated democracy within its ranks, support for military trade unions and/or for independent republic/new state force structures.[104] Those most insistent on such themes, such as Lopatin and General Konstantin Kobets of the General Staff, were encouraged to find new homes. Lopatin became Russian President Yeltsin's chief military advisor, Kobets his 'defence minister in waiting'.

The army was not wedded to establishment ideology, though (in 1990) 75 per cent of officers were Party members, and another 15 per cent were members of the Komsomol, the Party's 'youth' wing. To most, the Party had symbolized patriotism. When the Party 'recommended' abrogation of article 6 of the Constitution, which had given it its monopoly on power in February 1990, the army was content to embrace successor symbols; 1990 saw military parades again blessed by Orthodox priests. The staff and role of the Military Political Administration, the army's 'political' arm, was cut by an initial 25 per cent (18 high-ranking officers were cashiered for corruption and incompetence).

The army would not fight for counterproductive ideological baggage. But it would fight for its memories, and sense of patriotism. The charge that Marshal Georgi Zhukov had risen through the ranks in the 1930s 'on the bodies of people he had denounced' was, perhaps, the last straw. The army rallied around the Karen Rash manifesto:

1991; available from author.

[103] Soviet Military Series #1; 1989–91: Transformation & Transition.

[104] Up to 40 per cent of Shchit members were demobilized as part of troop reductions in 1990; Mark Galeotti, 'Civil Society in Uniform', *Russia and the World*, p 17 (1990).

the military should feel they are the background and sacred institution of a thousand years (of) statehood... At the turning points in history, the military proved the main, real hope of the people and frequently fulfilled assignments that at first glance appeared inappropriate...Thus Peter I ordered in 1722 that the military run the Orthodox Church...Zhukov is the embodiment of the 'Soldier as Russian Patriot'.[105]

The army accepted the need for change, and, in particular, the need to adjust to new fiscal realities (see below), but it preferred managed change, and it preferred 'centrist' change. Early reform focused on two domains.

The first concerned the character of tomorrow's army, and whether to retain conscription or embrace, rather, the concept of a purely voluntary 'professional' force. Proponents for the latter favoured the British or American example; they found prominent advocates, from both military and civilian ranks.[106] Opponents referred to Russia's traditional 'school of the nation' concepts, and French philosopher Jean-Jacques Rousseau's reported admonishment: 'those who rely on mercenaries deserve to be slaves'; they echoed the arguments of the Swedish reformers who pioneered the conscription route in reaction to the rogue armies of their day--to ensure social representativeness and thus, they thought, societal control. They argued that the cost of a purely professional army would be prohibitive, and that its vaunted advantages were in any case illusory; they pointed to the professionalism of conscript armies (with contract cores) such as those of Germany, Norway or Switzerland.

The end result (crystallized after the failed coup of August 1991) was a compromise, weighted toward the latter models. Conscription would be retained, to safeguard mobilization prospects, but the percentage of the cohort that was actually called up would be limited--initially, as in Poland, to 25 per cent. Conscription would be cut to 18 months (24 for naval service) with liberal alternative service and amnesty provisions. The professional core, serving on three to five year contracts (after successful graduation from a six-month military school), would be expanded to a peacetime norm of 75 per cent within five to seven years--though this aspiration was finance-dependent. The initial target of the Russian Defence Ministry established early in 1992 was 50 per cent.[107]

---

[105] Karen Rush, 'The Army and Culture', *Voenno-Istoricheskii Zhurnal* (January–April 1989).

[106] See report on Deputy Air Defence Commander General V. Andreyev's advocacy of a 'professional army', *FBIS-SOV 91-213*; and 'Renegade Russians Grab for Military Control' (on Lopatin proposals), *The Bulletin of the Atomic Scientists* (January, February 1991).

[107] *New Times* (Moscow) October 1991; see also *Izvestia*, 14 September 1991, and *Report on the USSR*, 25 October 1991; also *RFE/RL Research Report*, 20 March 1992.

The formula promised heretofore unknown Russian ethnic homogeneity. (This was already emerging, *de facto*: 1991 draft fulfilment ranged from 100 per cent in the RSFSR, Belorussia and Azerbaijan to 12.3 per cent in Lithuania and 8.2 per cent in Georgia; the proportion of native Russian speakers had already risen from a low of 42 per cent in 1989 to 66.5 per cent in 1990.[108]) It also promised a healthier, more selectively recruited army.[109]

The second initial reform domain concerned electoral accountability. Former Secretary General Leonid Brezhnev's governmental formula of job stability and allowing each functional branch of society maximum authority in its domain, a reaction to Khrushchev's constant reorganization and personnel turnover, contributed directly to the ossification, stagnation and corruption that ultimately doomed the regime. Its effect on the military may not have been as dire, because external challenges (such as Afghanistan) forced constant reevaluations, and because newly established civilian think tanks, notably the Academy of Sciences Institute for the USA and Canada (founded in 1967), provided alternative sources for security analysis and threat evaluation. Nevertheless, the General Staff crucially acted as *de facto* Secretariat to the supreme Defence Council (chaired by the Secretary General of the Party), and thus did control to a large extent the agenda and presentation of issues.

In 1989 other actors with formal rights of input were established: a new Department of Arms Control and National Security within the Party Central Committee (headed by General Alexander Starodubov of the GRU, it drew its staff from Defence, Foreign Affairs and the Academy of Sciences); a new arms control, disarmament and national security planning body within the Ministry of Foreign Affairs (headed by Victor Karpov); and an expanding Committee of Soviet Scientists for Peace, now renamed the Committee of Soviet Scientists for Global Security (co-chaired by Andrey Kokoshin, Deputy Director of the Institute for the USA and Canada, and Director of the Soviet Committee for the Monitoring of Unilateral Arms Reductions). Defence Council membership, previously restricted to the Secretary General (and Commander-in-Chief), the two or three Party Secretaries and Politburo members with immediate responsibilities in defence-related fields and the Minister of Defence, the Chief of the General Staff and the Chairman of the KGB, now swelled close to twenty. It was given a civilian secretariat, which received input from all of the above. It

---

[108] *Jane's Intelligence Review* (February 1992).

[109] Note *inter alia* M. Feshbach and S. Dorman, 'Demography, Nationality and Soviet Military Recruitment Problems', in D.R. Jones (ed.), *Proceedings of the Third Bedford Colloquium on Soviet Military-Political Affairs*, The Russian Research Centre of Nova Scotia, 1992.

was in effect being transformed into something akin to Washington's National Security Council.[110]

Other changes in 1989–90 also evoked the US model. The newly elected Supreme Soviet appointed a Committee on Defence and State Security, with Subcommittees on Defence and Armed Services, Defence Industry, and State Security. With help from an experts' group drawn largely from Kokoshin's 'shop', the former, under its chairman Evgenii Velikhov, established procedures for annual presentation and vetting of defence budgets and policy. In late summer 1989 it authorized Kokoshin to negotiate an agreement with Les Aspin, then chairman of the House Armed Services Committee in Washington, that would see each body invite the other side to respond to the threat spectrum presented in their defence ministries' annual 'posture statements'.[111]

Gorbachev's new Supreme Soviet-based presidency also established an American-style Chief of Staff position; Vladimir Lukin was appointed Chief of the Scientific and Analytical Staff of the Office of the Chairman of the Supreme Soviet. Lukin, a former colleague of Kokoshin at the Institute for the USA and Canada, had transferred to the Foreign Ministry under Eduard Shevardnadze, serving first as deputy director of its Far East division, and then as director of long range planning. However, the nature of his new position as originally envisioned fell victim to Gorbachev's move to a self-sustaining presidency with a larger presidential council of senior advisors. This, in turn, was transformed in November 1990 into a 'super-cabinet' Council of the Federation, made up of the Soviet President (its chairman), Republic Presidents, and the chairmen of the Supreme Soviet and its two chambers. Lukin, in the meantime, was elected to the new Russian parliament, in April 1990. He became chairman of its Foreign Affairs Committee, with primary responsibility for Russia's negotiations with other republics--the attempt to weave a new foundation for the confederation of the future.[112]

The 1989-90 elections of separatist movements and governments in a number of republics, from the Baltics to Georgia, reflected the accelerating dynamic of galloping, exclusive and centrifugal nationalisms, riding the crest of socioeconomic alienation, and testing and challenging the declining authority of the centre. They doomed Gorbachev's vision of a social democratic successor federation, and dictated the much more decentralized

---

[110] See C.G. Jacobsen, 'Dramatic Changes in Soviet Defence Decisionmaking', *Bulletin of Peace Proposals*, PRIO/SAGE, June 1990; and 'Soviet Defence Decisionmaking in Flux: A Postscript', *BPP*, March 1991.

[111] *Ibid.*

[112] *Ibid.*

essence of his final effort to engineer a looser confederacy of states, with central authority restricted to security, fiscal and foreign policies.

Public concern was manifest, and rising. Tatyana Zaslavskaya's All-Union Centre for the Study of Public Opinion on Socio-Economic Questions found that three-quarters of respondents wanted 'firm order in the country, stability and confidence in the future' (though there was no apparent consensus on how these motherhood and apple pie aspirations should be implemented); 10 per cent wanted return to the Stalinist system. Calls for 'stability of laws...continuity of obligations...and protection against crime and social disturbance', and admonitions that these are equally crucial 'in a market economy', proliferated.[113] In January 1991 *Izvestia* concluded: 'An increasing number of people can be prompted to think that a firm hand is the only way to firm order'.[114]

The conservative and chauvinist momentum was reflected in the establishment of a second 'independent' military union, the Russian Arms Union, which advocated a 'sovereign, democratic Russia with a strong Russian(!) executive'.[115] But the preference and sentiment of the military leadership, accustomed to equating Russian and Soviet interests, were most graphically displayed in May interviews with Oleg Baklanov, First Deputy Chairman of the Defence Council, and Rodionov, now Commander of the General Staff Academy, and in a hard-line July manifesto, 'A Word to the People', signed by General V. Varennikov (Commander in Chief of Soviet Ground Forces), Gromov and others.[116]

They attacked those 'who do not love their country'; the state [is] 'sinking into non-existence...Our home is already burning to the ground...[We will not] allow a fratricidal war or the destruction of the Fatherland'. Baklanov emphasized that 'enormous organizational experience has been accumulated in the armed forces and defence industry of which society can take advantage...[They have] demonstrated ability to create an entire economy [and have] much greater organizational experience than...newly appointed politicians who are incapable of ensuring even garbage collection on the streets of Moscow, cannot feed or clothe the population, or plan a city management strategy'. Rodionov maintained: 'Despite the...anti-army uproar, the army remains the people's favourite...[They] have developed a certain scepticism towards many structures, but not toward the army.'

---

[113] *Literaturnaya Gazeta*, 12 September 1990.

[114] *Izvestia*, 18 January 1991.

[115] *Report on the USSR*, 24 May 1991.

[116] *Sovietskaya Rossia*, 23 July 1991; see also article (from *Jane's Intelligence Review)* in *The Globe & Mail*, 20 August 1991.

The August coup plotters had reason for confidence. The army appeared to have expressed its support. Gromov's signature to the July manifesto presumably gave confidence to his Minister, Boris Pugo, a central member of the Emergency Committee (he later committed suicide). Achalov, the Deputy Defence Minister charged with combating public disturbance, and thus defence liaison with Gromov, may or may not have been responsible for the earlier Vilnius crackdown (see above). But as Commander of Airborne Forces, his previous post, he had orchestrated a pre-November Revolution Day exercise in Moscow that appeared designed to show his troops' readiness to answer a call to 'duty'; his Minister, Dmitrii Yazov, another Committee member, must have felt equally assured.

Yet their assurance was misplaced. The *Afghantsy*, crucially, did not go along.[117] When his Minister joined the August plotters, surely assuming activation of Gromov's special forces security troop network, Gromov gave the contrary signal of no signal--this was not the emergency for which he had prepared; the Moscow *Omon* organized the defence of the 'White House', the Russian parliament, and Yeltsin. Lieutenant-General (later General of the Army) Pavel Grachev, Achalov's successor as Airborne Assault commander, had been Gromov's First Deputy in Afghanistan; with Gromov he had successfully orchestrated the last large-scale operation of the war--breaking the siege of Khost. Like Gromov, he was awarded Hero of the Soviet Union. Now he joined Colonel-General Evgenii Shaposhnikov, the Air Force Commander-in-Chief, who threatened to bomb the Kremlin if the putschists did not surrender. The Commander of the KGB's elite *Alpha* assault unit (General Karpukhin, another Afghan veteran) also refused the call, as did the *Vitebsk* KGB airborne division.[118]

They were not the most senior *refusniks*; those were General Yuri Maximov, Commander-in-Chief of the Strategic Rocket Troops, Admiral Vladimir Chernavin, Commander-in-Chief of the Navy, and General Vladimir Lobov, the former Warsaw Pact Commander, who was to become Chief of the General Staff. Others effectively stood down, notably Chief of the General Staff, General Michail Moiseev, whose promotion by Gorbachev to Defence Minister was rescinded by Yeltsin. Some army and navy units answered the putschists' call, accepting their claim to legitimacy. But, under the circumstances, none did or could take decisive action. The *Afghantsy* were the shock troops, so to speak. They decided the outcome. There is no doubt that Yeltsin, Sobchak and others

---

[117] See also 'The Role of the Security Forces', *Report on the USSR*, 6 September 1991.

[118] For a good early analysis see G. Jukes, 'Younger military leaders reflect new political philosophy', *Asia-Pacific Defence Reporter*, November 1991.

of the opposition would have been arrested or worse in short order had they decided differently.[119]

The fascinating question is: why? They had been prepared to answer a call by Gorbachev (Gromov's ties to Gorbachev can be traced to his time as Commander of a Motor Rifle Regiment in the North Caucasus, 1975–78; Gorbachev was a member of the District Military Council).[120] Yet they were not prepared to defend less certain legitimacy; they were not prepared to prop up a now widely discredited ideology and largely de-legitimized system. They were conservative rather than liberal, and contemptuous of the apparent incompetence of many democratic politicians. But they were ready to transfer their sense of patriotism to another banner, that of Russia. The urgent, pleading, defiant and ultimately persuasive voice of Russian Vice President Rutskoi (another member of the *Afghantsy* brotherhood!), on radio *Ekho*, clearly had a bearing on events.

In the immediate aftermath of the failed coup the *Afghantsy* faded from public eye. The limelight was on leadership cleansing. With the appointment of Shaposhnikov as Minister of Defence came the stated intention to retire 80 per cent of the officer corps. Lobov charted 'radical reform'--with the emphasis on united structure and firm, central (and civilian) control.[121]

But disagreement quickly surfaced, both with regard to the meaning of the formula, and the mechanics of its implementation. Lobov was soon persuaded that more autonomous republic/new state military structures must be accommodated before they could be coopted into a 'system of regional and international security' that would ensure 'the country's nationwide security on the basis of the preservation and radical restructuring of its single military-political space'; the new states should replace, *de facto* as well as *de jure*, the old military districts (except in Central Asia, where local conditions were seen to dictate, rather, a regional composite); the general staff should be the supreme military coordinating body, with direct access to the highest civilian authority.[122] Shaposhnikov, however, continued to insist on 'unified armed forces', with status-of-forces agreements negotiated between the centre and individual republics--a federate rather than confederate model, and with the centre (Commonwealth of Independent States) Ministry of Defence as its apex. Lobov was

---

[119] Soviet Military Series # 1: 1989-91; also the *New York Times*, 23 August 1991.

[120] *Ibid*. Gorbachev had been a member since 1969.

[121] *Komsomolskaya Pravda*, 10 September 1991; also *New York Times*, 1 September 1991.

[122] Jacob Kipp, 'The Uncertain Future of the Soviet Military, From Coup to Commonwealth: The Antecedents of National Armies', *European Security*, Summer 1992, 207-338; *Krasnaya Zvezda*, 23 October 1991.

compelled to retire, for 'health reasons', in December 1991.[123] A few months later, however, Russia's decision to emulate Ukraine and the more assertively sovereignist New States in establishing its own distinct armed forces organization and structure effectively vindicated Lobov's confederate course.[124] It also set the stage for yet another 'generational' passing of the baton, the second in less than a year. This time, the *Afghantsy* were direct beneficiaries.

At the end of the process of retirements, reassignments and review (and propelled also by the dynamic and political impact of unfolding events), 'five of the top seven Russian Defence Ministry posts have been filled by former commanders in Afghanistan'; by the following year the *Afghantsy* were also playing a dominant role in the formulation of doctrine (see below).[125]

Moscow and the 'Near Abroad'

From Revolution Unleashed to New Successor State(s). The real revolution unleashed was of course sparked by what in hindsight is most accurately described as the second, successful coup when, with Gorbachev at the Russian parliamentary lectern after his return from Crimean house arrest, and under the glare of TV lights, Yeltsin banned the Communist Party with the flourish of a pen--and proceeded to dictate the composition of the government. Gorbachev's power was emasculated. The act unleashed the last remaining fetters holding the forces of galloping nationalism. It unleashed the forces of separatism, and hasty Western recognition--often extended with little appreciation for either the territorial entities or the nature of the governments that were recognized. Lithuania, for example, had been expanded and given Vilnius (today's capital) and regions with Russian and Polish populations by Stalin as salve for absorption; Khrushchev had given Russian-majority Crimea to the Ukraine without even a nod to the legal requirement of Supreme Soviet ratification; the Uzbek government that proclaimed democratic independence supported the coup, and proclaimed independence only in order to preserve old power structures.

The rush to dissolution, the engendered fears of 'Yugoslavias' writ large, the attempt to construct and maintain a successor confederacy, attendant internal and external security dynamics, and the later emergence of a more assertive, nationalist Russia and a new military doctrine will be discussed later. But, first, a focus on economic underpinnings.

---

[123] Kipp, 'Uncertain Future'.

[124] *Krasnaya Zvezda*, 14 April 1992; 'we [must] first divide and then unite'.

[125] *RFE/RE Research Report*, 21 August 1992, 9.

Economic problems; military–civilian conversion; arms sales. The cost and immensity of the withdrawals from empire--Afghanistan, East Europe and Mongolia--quickly burst the budget. Gorbachev's projected 14.2 per cent cut became six per cent in the first year.[126] The beginning of price liberalization and consequent rising prices did not help. The 1991 defence budget of 96.6 billion roubles was 36 per cent higher than in 1990, but had less purchasing power.[127]

As mentioned, Gorbachev's 'new industrial' civilian economic structures and agencies drew proven managerial experience from military industry. Yet such management alone proved insufficient, without the context of that industry's discipline. Soon new civilian ventures were moved under the military-industrial umbrella.[128]

The removal of the bureaucratic divide between military and civil industry did not remove the legacy of advantage. According to Vice President Rutskoi, in 1991 the military employed 80 per cent of the country's scientific expertise; military industry represented half the national income; the purchasing power of the defence rouble was four to five times higher than that of the civilian rouble; its relative advantage was reflected in the fact that military industry was the only sector in the economy to over fulfil consumer production targets.[129] Clearly this chasm between the two spheres needed to be bridged.

Meanwhile, the logic of relative advantage showed. About 40 per cent of military-industrial output had gone to the civilian sector, at least since the 1960s; its more advanced production facilities had always been relied on for a wide range of civilian products, from refrigerators and TVs to photographic equipment, computers and video systems (however primitive by the standards of some). At the end of 1991 defence industries produced 3000 types of consumer goods, worth 13.5 billion roubles, with a significant proportion destined for export (the degree to which military industry is also a crucial 'civilian' exporter is all too

---

[126] *Aviation Week & Space Technology* [hereafter *AW&ST*], 3 June 1991.

[127] *Ibid.*

[128] Julian Cooper, 'Management of the Defence Industry: the Soviet Union', in Jacobsen (ed.) *Strategic Power*.

[129] *Moscow News*, #39 (1991), and *Radio Rossii*, 6 March 1992 (re consumer production targets); for in-depth background information and analysis see C.G. Jacobsen (ed.), *The Soviet Defence Enigma: estimating costs and burden* (Oxford 1987).

often unappreciated in the West).[130] By 1989 the civilian percentage of military-industrial output had risen to 50 per cent; a year later it approached 60 per cent.[131] By 1992, with defence procurement, research and development slashed (down about two-thirds from 1991 levels), the figure rose to 80 per cent.[132] Amidst real and sometimes successful pressures to diversify and privatize, and overall economic decline, defence industry assets increased.[133]

It was typical and symptomatic that when Moscow's Department of Energy and Energy Efficiency in 1993 began the task of 'making the city's plethora of factories and power stations fuel efficient, energy conscious operations', it was to defence industries that they turned—to develop:

> heat meters, (equipment) to check energy consumption levels, electricity meters, new building insulation...a super-strong glue for pipe repairs, an experimental heat pump, and an automated system for boiler operations.[134]

Defence industries were not unaffected by the general phenomenon of New State barriers and tariffs severing traditional supply lines (component manufacturing was usually provided by one monopoly; it was normal for different components to be made in different republics). In the defence sector such fracturing was less severe than in many others. The 'share of the Russian Federation' ranged from 67 per cent of the total number of defence enterprises to 90.2 per cent of research and development.[135] This conferred bargaining levers. In view also of the fact that this sector maintained distinct all-(ex-)Union ties and presence, through 'Commonwealth' sanction and/or through 'all-Union' Officers Assemblies and other networks, New State restrictions could often be circumvented.

Early efforts to convert to civilian purpose the excess capacity caused by rock bottom military procurement (the nuclear sphere, cut 39.3 per cent, was partially exempt, but overall procurement shrank to just 2.9 per cent of total military expenditures) were, in fact,

---

[130] *Moscow Radio*, 10 August 1991; exact export percentages are unclear, but the fridge figure of 40 per cent may be representative.

[131] *Moscow Radio*, 18 October 1991.

[132] *Moscow Interfax*, 13 October 1991; also *AW&ST*, 27 January 1992, and *RFE/RL Research Report*, 14 August 1992.

[133] *Izvestia*, 9 September 1991; see also *International Defence Review,* 7 (1991).

[134] M. Miscavage, 'Keeping Russian Industry', *Moscow Tribune* (Business/Finance), early July 1993.

[135] 'Defence Complex of ex-USSR and Russian Federation', Moscow News, 9 (1992).

unimpressive.[136] A tank factory might build prams, or demonstrate a tank's ability to haul harvesters, but this was scarcely a cost-effective use of factory capacity, the trained workforce or, indeed, the tank. So also with artillery shells remade into lamps.[137] And if such output still appeared cost-effective when compared to civilian industries, this said more about the prospects of the latter than those of the former. In fact, military industries converted to civilian production saw their output fall by 30 per cent in 1991, and another 30 per cent in 1992.[138] The military faced a growing unemployment problem, in its industries as in its fighting and support formations.[139]

At the same time defence spending continued to fall in real terms, by six per cent a year. Overall military investment dropped 33 per cent (one estimate went as high as 50 per cent) in 1991, though high technology investment escaped the chopping block; it was protected.[140] Conversion costs were estimated at US $150 billion; arms exports, with a hoped-for $10 billion annual potential, appeared the most promising source of funding.[141] Overall exports were down, for the fourth year in a row. GNP shrank by 12 per cent in the first nine months of 1991; industrial production was down 6.4 per cent.[142]

Privatization was scarcely the issue. Defence industries suffered the same prospect as other heavier industry; the only conceivable outside buyers were corrupt ex-party *nomenklatura*, or the mafia (whose primary purpose was the laundering and legitimizing of ill-gotten gain), or foreign suitors, who tended to be ruled out for reasons of security. Military industry management teams chose instead, as did most of their more successful

---

[136] *RFE/RF Research Report*, 10 April 1992; *International Defence Review*, 7 (1991). Submarine production, for example fell from ten in 1990 to four in 1991. Downsizing was also evident in faster retirement rates.

[137] *Kommersant*, 2 March 1992.

[138] *Tass*, 29 February 1992.

[139] *Ibid.* Conversion efforts were expected to cause the lay-off of one million workers by mid-1992. See also V.S. Ritter, 'Soviet Defence Conversion', *Problems of Communism*, September/October 1991; A. Alexander, 'The Conversion of Soviet Defence Industry', *RANDP7620*, Santa Monica, CA, January 1990; and K. Ballantyne, 'Soviet Defence Industry Reform: the problems of conversion in an unconverted economy', *CIIPS Background Paper* # 9 136, Ottawa, July 1991.

[140] *Moscow News*, 9 (1992); Jane's Defence Weekly, 7 March 1992.

[141] 'Restructuring of Defence Proves Problematic', *Moscow News*, 9 (1992).

[142] *Jane's Defence Weekly*, 1 February 1992.

civilian counterparts, effectively to privatize themselves.[143] Now operating under far looser central strictures and control than before, and increasingly appreciative of the advantages and potential that this entailed, they began to transform their associations and combines into 'big business'. As such, they opposed divestiture--opposing sell-off of any part that either was or might prove profitable. Their favoured solution was cooperation with other big business at home and, in sharp reversal of earlier bias, with those abroad; they also favoured a more concerted arms sales effort, if necessary encompassing state-of-the-art technologies not previously made available to foreign clients.

Conversion remained essential, yet conversion enterprises lost 3.3 billion roubles in 1991, while the cushioning all-Union stabilization fund disappeared. It was also painfully slow, not least because of the costs involved. By mid-1991, out of 3500 defence production facilities, only 422 were in the conversion programme, of which only 56 were due to be entirely converted to civilian output; total conversion had in fact been completed in only five cases.[144] A year later brought the assertion that 'every military plant in Russia is undergoing some conversion', though only ten per cent were scheduled to convert 80-100 per cent of their output; the schedule, funds permitting, was implementation over 15 years.[145]

Again, the preferred solution was 'cooperation in...conversion between the Defence Ministry and enterprises in our military-industrial complex and Western partners' (especially German and US), and high technology arms sales.[146] Anatolii Volsky, Head of the Industrial and Scientific Union which spearheaded the 'industrialists' lobby', noted that although COCOM, the Western list of proscribed high technology exports, had been relaxed, it still effectively thwarted prospects of Western aid to the conversion effort.[147] Nevertheless, Moscow's Institute for the US and Canada and Stanford University's Centre for International Security and Arms Control did succeed in helping to coordinate a variety of joint US-Soviet business ventures, especially in defence; by mid-1991 600 Soviet defence industry concerns were exploring exports and alternative technological applications.[148] Kokoshin, who was also one of the more important 'midwives' behind this effort, listed Soviet strengths and primary

---

[143] *Kommersant*, 2 March 1992, for reports on the MIC joint stock company *Kolo*'s attempt to effect the 'illegal act' of 'nomenklatura-led privatization'.

[144] *Tass*, 20 December 1991; *International Defence Review*, 7 (1991).

[145] *RFE/RL Research Report*, 14 August 1992; *Reuters*, 7 May 1992.

[146] *Izvestia*, 20 October 1991 (quoting General K. Kobets).

[147] *Le Monde*, 10 September 1991.

[148] *AW&ST*, 2 September 1991.

sales prospects: space technology, rocket building, aviation industry, ship building, high quality steel and composite materials, (some) oil production and oil rig equipment, and laser technology.[149]

The new Yeltsin government sanctioned aggressive arms sales; Rutskoi would oversee the effort; 50 per cent of arms sales exports would go to subsidizing the costs of conversion.[150] By late 1991 arms sales had become the *sole* source of funding for conversion, and a crucial contributor to the extraordinary housing construction programme necessitated by troop withdrawals.[151] The Law on Conversion of Defence Industries of March 1992 established a new conversion fund from enterprise contributions, but this (and related foreign investment--$300 million by May 1992) remained grossly inadequate. Mikhail Malei, Yeltsin's presidential counsellor on conversion, noted bluntly: Russia 'cannot afford to be more scrupulous than others, say the US or France, in selling arms in international markets'.[152] The only question concerned the distribution of sales income, whether it was to be spread equally to all claimants. Malei thought the 40 per cent most competitive enterprises, those able to sell their products abroad, should subsidize the remaining 60 per cent. Kokoshin advocated from whom to whom; to maximize investment efficiency available funds should go primarily to those who proved able to compete, be they military or civilian exporters.[153]

Released from bureaucratic interference, defence industry and science were told to achieve self-sufficiency.[154] They were also charged implicitly with the task of ensuring against an uncontrolled brain drain of defence scientists.[155] US and EEC concern that some nuclear scientists, in particular, might find their way to the highest bidder led to some subsidization--notably US funding for 100 nuclear fusion researchers in Moscow.[156] Yet such aid remained strictly limited (between one and two thousand Soviet scientists were thought

---

[149] *Krasnaya Zvezda*, 17 March 1992.

[150] *Ibid.*; also *Moscow News*, 7 (1992), on government decree giving defence industry free access to foreign markets; and *Izvestia*, 22 February 1992.

[151] *Rossiiskaya Gazeta*, 28 February 1992.

[152] *Reuters,* 7 May 1992.

[153] *ITAR-TASS*, 8 April 1992.

[154] *Moscow News*, 26 (1991).

[155] *Komsomolskaya Pravda*, 27 November 1991.

[156] *New York Times*, 6 March 1992.

to have the skills necessary to design nuclear weapons), not least due to concern that it did also constitute *ipso facto* the shoring up of a weakened but still very potent competitor.[157] Moscow clearly appreciated that this aid could be no more than a limited, short term palliative.

New production, promotion and sales alliances emerged, complementing the few that already existed, such as *Glavkosmos*, established in 1985 to promote space commercialization, and now marketeer for joint Russian-Kazakh space launch services (employing SS-25 boosters) and potential seller of SS-18 and SS-24 ICBMs.[158] *Skorost*, designed to amalgamate Yakovlev and other aircraft design and manufacturing efforts, *Dianond*, another combine of research and production facilities seeking optimization of profits and opportunities, *Navycon*, a naval share-holding company whose subsidiaries are joint stock companies of the fleets, and other military joint stock companies pursuing investment, conversion and communications prospects spearheaded the new trends.[159]

The former Flight Control Centre in Kaliningrad was converted into a stock exchange for military industries; it later amalgamated with some of the other military-industrial exchanges that soon sprouted (including *Konversiya* and *ESTRA*), to form the Military-Industrial Bureau, to trade specialized instruments and materials, electronics, chemical, metallurgical and construction industry products for consumer goods.[160] Limited military-industrial stock offerings were now apparently available to foreign investors.[161] Direct foreign investment was also welcomed. General Electric and Snecma (its French partner) agreed to invest in PS90 turbofan engine production and development, in Perm; India negotiated involvement in the development of the first supersonic VTOL, the Yak-141, and its R-79 engine; Sukhoi sought investors for its Su-37 multi-role combat plane.[162]

Rolls-Royce entered into partnership with Tupolev to provide British engines and American avionics to the new medium range Tu-204 (this 214 passenger competitor to

---

[157] *New York Times*, 1, 23, 28 March 1992; *AW&ST*, 20 January 1992.

[158] *Jane's Intelligence Review*, March 1992; *AW&ST*, 14 October 1991 and 20 January 1992.

[159] *AW&ST*, 18 November 1991, on aerospace enterprises' pursuit of alliances at home and abroad; *Moscow Radio*, 2 November 1991; *Tass*, 20 December 1991.

[160] *Izvestia*, 4 July 1991; *Ekonomika i zhizn*, 27 (July 1992); *RFE/RL Research Report*, 31 July 1992.

[161] *FBIS-SOV 91-212*, 1 November 1991; one military-industrial investment firm put ten per cent of its stock up for sale.

[162] 'Russian Engine Firms Strive to Realign', *AW&ST*, 30 March 1992; *International Herald Tribune*, 7 September 1992.

Boeing 757 and Airbus A-340, was launched at the June 1993 Paris Air Show) and later models.[163] Pratt & Whitney signed and later extended (joined by Collins Avionics of Rockwell International) a joint engine-avionics-airframe venture with the Ilyushin Design Bureau and other Russian suppliers and components manufacturers, offering aid-to-certification and global marketing of Russian planes, titanium sponge, semi-products and finished parts. The first result, a $700 million sale of 320 seat Il-96s to Partnairs, a Dutch leasing company, was announced in June 1993.[164] France's Groupe Snecma joined with Mikoyan, grafting Larzac engines and Snecma's servicing reputation to the MiG AT, to produce up to 600 advanced military training jets for Russian and foreign forces.[165] Meanwhile, Dowty/Smiths Industries of the UK married FADEC (full-authority digital engine controls) to a Ukrainian/Russian engine design, thus further improving prospects also for Russian engine manufacturers.[166]

The merger of perhaps the most dynamic rocket developers and manufacturers (in part because overambitious, competitive marketing threatened necessary cooperation) into the 'first Russian rocket-space firm' occurred in 1993. They were the design office *Salyut* and the *Khrunichev* research and production centre, the developers and marketers of the Proton (UR-500K) launcher. The former had already 'concluded contracts for the development of rocketry with the Indian organization for space research, the German aerospace agency DARA, the firm DASA and with the international organization Inmaisat for launching a communication satellite'. The latter had signed contracts with Motorola for three Proton launchings, and with Lockheed 'for the sale of its rockets on the world market'. The amalgamation was expected to secure launch contracts with Immarsat, Intelsat, Eutelsat and Asiasat, the right to launch at least 12 American satellites before the end of the decade-- and perhaps a far larger number (negotiations proceeded on Motorola's planned 66-satellite global cell phone network)--and increase the number of geostationary satellites by at least a third.[167] The indirect pairing of the Indian space agency and Lockheed ultimately ran afoul of US laws, with some damage to Russia's reputation for reliability--offset by confirmation of its commercial priorities, and improved prospects for COCOM bypass (see below).[168]

---

[163] *RFE/RL Research Report,* 28 August 1992.

[164] *Economist,* 19 June 1993.

[165] *International Herald Tribune,* 12-13 June 1993.

[166] *AW&ST,* 13 April 1992.

[167] *Moscow News,* 2 July 1993; *Economist,* 20 February 1993.

[168] *Ibid.*

Soviet and later Russian military hardware-for-sale exhibitions were held at home and abroad. The Conversion-91 exhibition in Bologna, Italy, for example, was said to have been a particular success, as were Mosaeroshow '92 in Moscow, the IDEX '93 defence exhibition in Abu Dhabi, and others--including the Farnborough Air Show and Le Bourget.[169] Items for sale included MiG 27, 29 and 31, Su 25TK (ground attack) and 27, Tu 22 bombers, Il 76 AWACS-type planes and aviation technologies.[170] The 'private' International Chetek Corporation of Moscow even offered peaceful nuclear explosion devices.[171]

By autumn 1991 all plane types were on offer, including the previously top secret 'wing-in-ground effect ekranoplane'; aircraft industry exports alone were now projected at US$70 billion over the next four to five years.[172] The Mi-26 heavy assault and Mi-28 attack helicopters were added to the list in 1992.[173] So also were the dual purpose 85 RU homing torpedo/anti-ship missile, the 3M-80 supersonic air-to-surface anti-ship missile ('vastly superior to any Western anti-ship missile currently in existence or even still on the drawing board'), the highly impressive S-300 anti-missile defence system (its six hits in six tries demonstration at the IDEX '93 defence exhibition in Abu Dhabi came as Israeli reviews downgraded the Patriots' Gulf War record to just one *possible* hit), and other state-of-the-art systems.[174] Once secret technologies now for sale also included a number of space advances said to be superior to their Western analogues--certain nuclear reactors, high strength high temperature alloys, space engines that use magnetic fields, and space stations.[175] US defence officials and industry expressed interest in (and began testing) a range of Soviet defence products, from advanced optics, engineered materials and high energy magnets to gallium arsenide--and the ekranoplane.[176]

---

[169] *Moscow News*, 39 (1991); *Military Technology*, 4 (1993). (Note the variety and quality of Russian defence industry advertisements!)

[170] *FBIS-SOV 91-160*, 19 August 1991; *Interfax*, 21 November 1991; *Guardian Weekly*, 3 November 1991, on offers of MiG 29 to the Pentagon for US$25 million each.

[171] *New York Times*, 7 November 1991.

[172] *AW&ST*, 18 November 1991; *Moscow News*, 43 (1991).

[173] *RFE/RL Research Report*, 28 August 1992.

[174] *Military Technology*, 4 (1993): 16-17, 64-9.

[175] *New York Times*, 4 November 1991.

[176] *AW&ST*, 19 August 1991; *International Defence Review*, 26 (September 1993): 685–703.

An initially negative US government decision, reflecting protectionist US space industry concern, was revised in February 1992, with negotiations proceeding on purchases of helicopters, selected anti-missile and advanced fuel rocket technologies, and nuclear space engines; France and other top-rank defence producers appeared equally interested.[177]

There remained deterrents to some potential sales. Western competitors assiduously spread the Gulf War 'lesson' of inferior Soviet arms, though the defeated, older vintage arms were scarcely representative of those now offered; some airframes were also judged too heavy, and hence fuel inefficient.[178] Aircraft, helicopter and missile sales were furthermore hampered by service and spare parts availability and delivery concerns.[179]

Sales values for 1991 were estimated at US$4-5 billion, including 553 tanks, 658 armoured vehicles and 1783 missiles of various types.[180] This was down dramatically from the *pro forma* highs of previous years (topped by $24.8 billion in 1986), yet those figures were unreal in that most sales then were noncommercial; furthermore, only a small portion of the payments that did accrue reached either military-industrial producers or other armed forces agencies.[181] Now most did.

Exports in 1992 were initially down significantly from 1991; 21 per cent of defence enterprises were said to be 'near bankruptcy'.[182] But a concerted sales effort turned the tide. Sales announced through the year included missile guidance technology, rocket engines, S-300 surface-to-air missiles with anti-missile capabilities, 24 SU-27 fighters (subject to ongoing bargaining: later reports spoke both of larger numbers and cancellation), 400 T-72 tanks, unspecified warships, tank, rocket and uranium enrichment technology, two 300 megawatt nuclear power plants to be completed over 12-13 years, and agreement-to-employ 200 Soviet scientists to China (China also expressed interest in purchasing the Varyag aircraft carrier being fitted out at Ukraine's Mikolaiv shipyards, with 22 Su-27, but this deal was not consummated); three diesel submarines, 110 planes, including SU-24 and MiG-27,

---

[177] See 'Star Wars Chiefs Want to Buy Soviet anti-Missile Advances', *New York Times*, 8 February 1992; *ibid.*, 19 February 1992; *Le Monde*, 10 February 1992; and *AW&ST*, 10 February, 30 March, 6 April and 2 November 1992.

[178] *AW&ST*, 18 November 1991.

[179] *Le Monde*, 18 December 1991.

[180] The Montreal *Gazette*, 26 September 1992 (from the *Independent*, London).

[181] *New York Times*, 21 July 1992; *RFE/RL Research Report*, 23 October 1992. (Malei estimated previous peak value at $14 billion, of which only $4-5 billion was cash.)

[182] *Krasnaya Zvezda*, 26 March 1992.

29 and 31 fighters, 12 Tu-22 bombers, 2 Il-76 AWACS and nuclear power plants to Iran; helicopters, armoured personnel carriers and rifles to Turkey (initiating a US$300 million arms sale package); T-72 tanks to Syria; SA-10 anti-air missiles to Libya; a Zhdanov cruiser, 30 MiG-29s, a ballistic missile rocket booster and missile technology to India (this latter deal, which proceeded despite US protest, and sanctions against *Glavkosmos*, was later terminated in return for greater-value access/sales to US space programmes--see above); two squadrons of MiG-29 fighters to Malaysia; combat jets to Saudi Arabia and Taiwan, for US$14.6 billion; infantry combat vehicles to Abu Dhabi; S-300 missiles and other weapons to the United Arab Emirates (they were also interested in Su-25TK ground attack planes); plus heavy lift helicopters to Pacific rim oil and other operators; finally, Indonesia expressed interest in Scud missiles; the Philippines in MiG-29s; and South Korea in S-300 missiles, multiple rocket launchers, Su-25 ground attack planes and Su-27 fighters.[183] Arms exports for 1992 were estimated at 10-12 billion dollars; there were also related natural resource sales, including uranium exports worth $800 million.[184]

In 1993 China's Su-27 purchase was confirmed (26 were bought), as was Thai interest in helicopters and, perhaps, MiG-31 high altitude interceptors, Malaysian in 'new technology to be used in the MiG-29', and other initiatives and follow-up.[185] Some sales appeared bargain-basement when compared to competitors' price structures, but market shares and inroads were gained, and production facilities saved (prior to the Chinese sale and South Korean interest, Sukhoi's Su-27 production line was down to two orders).

Chinese purchases and increased Russian-Chinese military-industrial cooperation were notable also in the years that followed. In 1994 China acquired SS-20 launch vehicles; in 1995 Russia agreed to Chinese co-production of the Su-27 (the initial production target was set at 200 planes), and began final negotiations on bomber upgrades.[186] Russia's larger sales effort, however, remained decidedly global in ambition, remarkably unrestricted and increasingly sophisticated.[187]

---

[183] 'Moscow is Selling Weapons', *New York Times*, 18 November 1991. See also *RFL/RL Research Report*, 6 March, 28 August, 4 and 25 September, 9 October and 18 December 1992; *AW&ST*, 9 March 1992; *Kyodo*, 4 May 1992; *Ottawa Citizen*, 17 May 1992; *IHT*, 7 September 1992; *Guardian Weekly*, 27 December 1992; also *New York Times*, 3 May and 23 June 1993; *Military Technology*, 4 (1993); and *International Defence Review*, September 1993.

[184] *RFE/RL Research Report*, 14 August 1992.

[185] *Moscow Tribune*, 7 and 9 July 1993; *Economist*, 17 July 1993.

[186] Confidential Chinese defence sources.

[187] See eg advertisement in *International Defence Review*, August 1995.

Minimal relief on the home front also appeared on the way. Government orders for military hardware were to increase by ten per cent in 1993; they would include a new medium range bomber, responding to the army's southern concern, and 'a fundamentally new, standardized missile of the next generation'.[188] The corner was turned. Yet new domestic orders, while providing relief to scientific/technical elites and employment prospects, would clearly not suffice, in and of themselves, to secure longer term viability. Foreign sales remained crucial.[189]

Many of these took the form of long term contracts. Deliveries remained and will remain below late Cold War averages. But, as noted above, these tended to be concessionary, to clients and allies. Post-1991 sales contracts were commercial (though sometimes with part-barter options that appealed to some buyers) and with no automatic or necessary restriction on purchasers. Traditionally Western arms markets were fair game--favoured game, in fact, in view of their generally superior credit.[190]

With energy and other traditional natural resource exports facing short and medium term prospects of decline or stagnation (they were shackled by a crumbling infrastructure, development of new extraction prospects lagging behind the depletion of old and/or jurisdictional wrangling about resource ownership and control), military industry exports in fact emerged as the single most important earner of convertible currency. It was also clearly more important than even the most illusory hope of Western aid and relief.

It was a potential that Moscow quite simply could not afford to blunt, despite Western concern. The expressed Western fear of destabilizing consequences in the Third World was in fact seen as hypocritical, and self-serving, in view of the West's own vigorous arms sales efforts.[191] In any case, Moscow could afford no other course.

*

The rush to dissolution; attempts at containment; external and internal security dynamics. In hindsight, Yeltsin's 'counter-coup' after the crumbling of the Emergency Committee in August 1991 was most remarkable for Gorbachev's resigned acceptance. As in Eastern Europe in 1989, when Gorbachev's preferred goal of forcing transition to

---

[188] *TAR-TASS*, 11 September 1992; *RFE/RL Research Report*, 27 November 1992.

[189] See Stephen Foye, 'Russian Arms Exports after the Cold War', *RFE/RL Research Report*, 26 March 1993; and Peter Almquist, 'Arms Producers Struggle', *RFE/RL Research Report*, 18 June 1993.

[190] *New York Times*, 18 October 1992.

[191] *Ibid*.

reformist governments of his own ilk failed, he could have commanded enough military and organizational loyalty to enforce his will; yet, when faced with the choice of brute force or abdication, he again chose the latter. It was, perhaps, his finest hour. But the choice also meant impotence. His authority was usurped. Formal dissolution of the old Union did not come until December. Real dissolution came quicker.

The Baltics declared independence, as did Russia(!), the Ukraine, and other Republics, and the momentum did not stop. 'Autonomous' regions declared independence from republics, and ethnic enclaves and even cities followed suit.

Galloping nationalism severed ties of economic logic, fuelling unemployment and inflation. By early November there were 20 million unemployed (many working unpaid); 80 per cent were women.[192] The unleashing of *laissez-faire* price and regulatory reform in January 1992 and their extension through subsequent months jolted these figures upward, fuelling the arguments of those who espoused order.[193] The nationalist beast also severed ties of military logic. Within six weeks the Ukraine and Kazakhstan had fudged pledges to be nuclear-free; 'their' missiles ranked them third and fourth among the world's powers. Azerbaijan 'annexed' Soviet forces on its soil, briefly becoming a nuclear power *de jure* (though not *de facto*); nuclear forces also remained on the territories of other new states.

Three arguments drove advocacy of a successor confederacy. The first derived from economic imperatives; nearly 80 per cent of the economy of the USSR was trans-republic (Russia was least dependent, yet for it also disruption of old ties was costly).[194] The second derived from concerns about nuclear security or, rather, the insecurities and dangers of diffusion. The third turned on the extraordinary ethnic mix of the old empire. Unlike British, French and other empires that could be easily disentangled, the Soviet/Russian was more like its Austro-Hungarian cousin, whose ethnic mix continues to reverberate; there are 25 million Russians with roots and homes in other successor states (11 million plus in the Ukraine alone), as well as millions of Ukrainians and other nationalities beyond the boundaries of 'their' new states.

Three counter-arguments propelled dissolution, and separatism. The first was nationalism--and its exclusive variety, which demanded rights for self not conceded to

---

[192] *CBC*, 'The Journal', 6 November 1991.

[193] See, for example, Jonathan Steele, 'Bitter and Betrayed' and 'Russian Right Unites against Yeltsin', *Guardian Weekly*, 16 February 1992, and 'Russia, right stuff, *Economist*, 29 February 1992; for more detailed coverage: 'Russian nationalism', CBC Radio feature report, 10 November 1991.

[194] For comparative statistics on inter-republic trade subsidization and dependence, see *Guardian Weekly*, 1 March 1992.

others. The second was reaction against decades or centuries of bureaucratic insensitivity to local concerns, and the perversions and mistakes that this engendered. The third argument, distinct yet intertwined, was the legacy of empire, of Moscow's on-again off-again attempts to Russify others (and, in the Soviet era, of analogous attempts by republican majorities, Georgian, Uzbek and others, to absorb 'their' ethnic minorities).

The Commonwealth of Independent States agreement, signed by Russia, Belarus and Ukraine and joined by Kazakhstan and others in December 1991, accepted the principles of economic common market and unified strategic command--but without all-Union authority. Gorbachev's insistence on minimal central powers was ignored. The head-less construction remained (and remains) mired in contradictions and uncertainty. There was no early agreement on monetary or fiscal policy, or on the structure or funding of other 'common' domains.

Through the autumn of 1991, in response to US President Bush's embrace of nuclear arms cuts, Gorbachev (supported by Yeltsin and the Republics) offered even sharper cutbacks.[195] Ukraine and others also agreed that nuclear warheads would be transferred to Russia--in part because this appeared the precondition for Western aid. By early 1992, however, harmony faltered. At the CIS summit in February, eight of the 11 agreed to a unified force (after two years). But Ukraine, Moldova and Azerbaijan refused. In March Ukraine suspended nuclear transfer because of professed concern about their fate in Russian hands; it still had 1420 strategic and 2390 tactical nuclear warheads.[196]

Yeltsin's post-coup comment that republics had the right to independence, but borders might then have to be redrawn, was subsequently muted. But the threat's withdrawal rested on the unspoken premise that Ukraine would subscribe to a looser union--as suggested by Ukrainian President Leonid Kravchuk's sponsorship of the Commonwealth. Hence the phenomenon (that autumn) that saw Russian leaders in Eastern Ukraine and the Crimea, including Admiral Kasatonov, Commander of the Black Sea Fleet, urge a yes vote in the referendum on Ukrainian independence: independence then meant Kravchuk and the Commonwealth; a no would lead to further radicalization and, ultimately, a more *independista* government. Hence, also, the later concern in Moscow when Kravchuk appeared intent on sabotaging the assumptions that underlay the Commonwealth; Gorbachev was among those who feared that, far from using independence as legitimizer for Commonwealth membership, Kravchuk was in fact using the latter to secure the former.

---

[195] See *New York Times*, 1 October 1991; and *Report on the USSR*, 25 October 1991.

[196] *Komsomolskaya Pravda*, 26 March 1992.

The question of a more separatist agenda intertwines with the separatist conundrum: nationalist passions made concessions to central authority career threatening (even on matters of obvious self-interest); yet without concessions there could be no central authority. And no fetters on republican independence meant no fetters on Russian independence; a Russia unfettered would always be more likely to have irredentist ambitions.

Ukraine was the crux--for its size and for its ethnic mix. The nationalist imperative was evident in its demand that ex-Soviet units swear allegiance to Kiev, its seizure of the army's main communication network in January 1992,[197] its demands for the transfer of the Black Sea Fleet, and its assertions of nuclear independence.[198] Yet change was sometimes less than apparent, and challenges were sometimes set aside rather than pursued.[199] Ukraine's rejection of a Commonwealth Army, for example, was followed 15 days later by a Kravchuk defence of cooperation with Russia; addressing a separatist audience, he noted that 'when there is frost on Thursday in Moscow, it reaches Kiev by Friday'.[200]

Nuclear uncertainties remained; Ukraine retained strategic air and missile capabilities, though tactical warheads were transferred over the summer. When Presidents Yeltsin and Bush signed START 2 in January 1991, Kiev's promised and necessary pre-requisite ratification of START 1 remained outstanding.[201] The potential for serious discord lessened, however, with the emergence of a state 'corporatist' consensus in Kiev, and the appointment in October 1992 of Leonid Kuchma as Prime Minister. (Kuchma was director of the missile production plant that developed the Soviet space shuttle.) The

---

[197] *New York Times*, 5, 9 January 1992. When Major General Bashkirov, the renegade commander of a CIS Strategic Air Division, refused to transfer to or, indeed, land at a Russian base, he was fired by Shaposhnikov, but 're-hired' by Kravchuk: *RFE/RL Research Report*, 6 March 1992.

[198] *Guardian Weekly*, 6 October 1991; *New York Times*, 23 October 1991; *FBIS-SOV 91-213*, 4 November 1991. Note also Natalia Feduschak (from Kiev), 'Ukraine may keep N-weapons', *Canadian Press*, 29 March 1992. Ukraine's lone refusal in March to commit to transfer of all nuclear arms to Russian soil by 1 July 1992 (for CIS disposal and/or destruction, as mandated by arms control agreements and IMF and other Western aid conditions), was presented as response to uncertainty concerning Russian dispositions, and not indicative of changed commitment: see *New York Times*, 1 April 1992.

[199] Ukraine's oath of allegiance was avoided by some (a number of air force and other mobile high technology units left for Russian soil) and ignored by others (*Tass*, 17 March 1992 report on the 'mutiny' of Lvov military school cadets); yet others acquiesced because it released pay and food--a commercial arrangement, rather than principle, buying conditional loyalty but no more.

[200] *Reuters*; *Montreal Gazette*, 29 February 1992.

[201] See, for example, *New York Times*, 3 January 1993.

consensus had ties to the 'industrialists' lobby' emergent in Moscow (see below).[202] Kuchma also had ties to Moscow's new defence elite--he knew Gromov, for example, from the latter's days as Kiev Military District Commander. Kuchma's later resignation proved a brief detour. His victory in the presidential election that followed confirmed the new ascendancy.

As separatist dynamics reached into Russia itself, Moscow initially looked inwards. Yeltsin voided the first independence declaration within Russia, by tiny Chechnya-Ingushetia in autumn 1991, and dispatched Interior Ministry troops. But they were withdrawn, by parliament, because of fear that an interventionist precedent could be used elsewhere to legitimize action against Russian minorities, and to assuage Ukrainian concern (prior to the then imminent referendum) that nascent Russian nationalism might precipitate divisive action beyond its currently defined state borders. Early caution was also reflected in the March 1992 decision to withdraw from Nagorno-Karabakh. There was neither military nor political stomach for involvement in others' conflict. Gromov, reappointed to his old Caucasian command for the purpose, repeated his Afghan exit.

Yet a somewhat more confident and assertive Russia was also emerging. Tatarstan's independence referendum on 21 March, Russia's second, also appeared the last. Although Moscow refrained from punitive measures, other than to declare the act illegal, the postscript was different. The next day Tatarstan's President was conciliatory, perhaps mindful of Chechnya's problems and dissipating resolve: 'Our first step will be...tighter union with Russia...new relations with a reformed Russia'; the referendum would save Russia, not destroy it.[203]

Nine days later, on 31 March 1992, Russia's remaining 84 regions signed a new union agreement, spelling out decentralization of powers, areas of joint jurisdiction, and areas under federal control--monetary policy, financial and currency regulation, the federal budget, energy distribution, nuclear power, defence and security.[204]

The next day, in response to attacks against the secessionist Russian-dominated Transdniestrian Moldovan Republic, Yeltsin decreed the ex-Soviet Fourteenth Army in Moldova to be Russian--denying jurisdiction to Moldova and the Commonwealth. Its Chief-of-Staff (Major-General Sitnikov) welcomed the decision, and declared readiness to act. It was Russia's first military intervention in support of its diaspora. This time parliament did not demur. The precedent was set.

---

[202] See *Economist*, 3, 17 October 1992.

[203] *New York Times*, 22 March 1992.

[204] *Nezavisimaya Gazeta*, 15 April 1992; also *Los Angeles Times*, 18, 19 April 1992.

The new course was reflected also in the final report of the parliament's Foreign Affairs Committee chaired by Lukin on the status of Crimea: its 1954 transfer to Ukraine had never been ratified, and was therefore illegal. The effort to shore up the Commonwealth as Soviet successor umbrella lost priority; 'Russia First' was the new creed. Lukin moved to Washington as Russia's new Ambassador. Russia's Defence Minister displaced Commonwealth Defence Minister Shaposhnikov in the ministry building in Moscow. The designation and shaping of Russia's new Defence Ministry was itself a signal event. When the idea of an independent Russian Army and Ministry was first muted, Marshal Shaposhnikov himself appeared the obvious candidate to many: he was young (born in 1942); he was a pilot (and thus a break also with the old leadership's army credentials); and had been Yeltsin's choice first as post-coup Soviet and later as Commonwealth Defence Minister. Other favoured choices included Lobov (succeeded as Chief of the General Staff by Leningrad MD Commander, General Victor Samsonov, in December 1991), Kobets, or Kokoshin, should a civilian be chosen.[205] In the end Kokoshin, whose inter-ethnic/state views parallel Lobov's, was made First Deputy Minister, and civilian liaison. But the Ministry went to Pavel Grachev and the *Afghantsy*.[206] They had saved Yeltsin during the August days. They also held high the banner of national and pan-national *Russian* interest.

Grachev brought Gromov back to Moscow, as the other First Deputy Defence Minister. Three other former Afghan commanders, Colonel-Generals Victor Dubynin, Valerii Mironov and Georgii Kondratev, were also brought in--giving five of the Ministry's top seven positions to Afghan veterans.[207]

They were distinguished by their youth; Grachev is six years younger than Shaposhnikov. And they were distinguished by the assertiveness of their patriotism. Grachev served notice that he 'would not allow the honour and dignity of Russians to be insulted on the territory of any other state'; Mironov affirmed that this duty to the diaspora extended to Russians in the Baltic.[208] In the west, Major-General Lebed, newly appointed Commander of the Fourteenth Army and also Afghan veteran, warned against 'fascist' Moldovan

---

[205] The Movement for Democratic Russia and Military for Democracy both recommended Kokoshin: see *RFE/RL Research Report*, 6 March 1992.

[206] Grachev described his appointment as a 'temporary compromise': see *RFE/RL Daily Report*, 22 May 1992.

[207] *Nezavisimaya Gazeta*, 11 June 1992.

[208] Stephen Foye, 'Post-Soviet Russia: Politics and the New Russian Army', *RFL/RL Research Report*, 21 August 1992.

attempts at genocide against the Russian population.[209] In the east, the general staff joined those who warned against territorial concessions to Japan before Yeltsin's planned visit to Tokyo (the visit was postponed); they followed up by directing the navy to reinforce Southern Kurile military units--a naval missile battalion on Iturup was to double its personnel and missile strength by 1993.[210] The ordered build-up was apparently rescinded later, but the political point was made.

Shaposhnikov followed suit by making it clear the CIS would neither need nor accept Western peacekeeping forces.[211] Black Sea Fleet vessels were sent off Abkhazia, disregarding protests by Ukraine and Georgia; the action underlined Moscow's rejection of Kiev's claim to the Fleet.[212]

The draft of a new military doctrine asserted Moscow's right to protect Russian-speaking minorities in Soviet successor states, with force if necessary, and to mount 'peacekeeping' operations (with the uncertain proviso that such action be approved by the Commonwealth).[213] This was a mandate the *Afghantsy* presumed.

The change also dealt with the nature of the new army. It was, of course, to be smaller; the Defence Law of 24 September 1992 decreed that numbers be capped at one per cent of the population by 1 January 1994.[214] The April Declaration on Priorities of Military Policy had already confirmed a conscript/volunteer mix. This was soon weighted towards the latter, spurred by conscript avoidance rates, which reached 95 per cent in Moscow and 70 per cent nationally in early 1993 (these were stemmed neither by the 1992 service cut from 24 to 18 months, nor the 1993 consideration of a further cut to 12 months), and disinclination to prosecute and convict. Promises of higher salaries and fringe benefits--housing, free transportation, uniforms and food--brought 110,000 accepted volunteers by

---

[209] *Sovietskaya Rossia*, 7 July 1992.

[210] *Interfax*, 18 August 1992; *RFL/RF Research Report*, 21 August 1992.

[211] *BBC*, 13 July 1992.

[212] *RFL/RL Research Report*, 3 April 1992: Kiev claimed 91 per cent of the Black Sea Fleet (its definition of the non-strategic component); CIS Naval Commander Admiral V. Chernavin (and Moscow) were willing only to transfer 20-22 per cent.

[213] See Stephen Foye, 'Post Soviet Russia', 12; and Scott McMichael, 'Russia's New Military Doctrine', *RFL/RL Research Report*, 9 October 1993.

[214] See A.A. Danilovich, 'On New Military Doctrines of the CIS and Russia', M.A. Gareev, 'On Military Doctrine and Military Reform in Russia', and C.J. Dick, 'Initial Thoughts on Russia's Draft Military Doctrine', in *Journal of Soviet Military Studies*, 5: 4 (December 1992).

September 1993, and plans for another 50,000 by year's end, 150,000 more in 1994, and a volunteer component of 50 per cent by year 2000. The armed forces would be recast.[215]

The Defence Law underlined the Russia First focus, with no mention of the CIS. The ultimate threat perceived was civil war; Article 10 provided legal basis, *in extremis*, for military assumption of government power. It noted that defensive forces *must* have offensive complements. Troops must be highly mobile.

Strategic forces had already been streamlined, as they downsized, into four components: the Strategic Rocket Troops, the Strategic Naval Forces, the Air Force and the Main Directorate of Space Systems, and apparently ranked in that order.[216] They were now assigned a 360-degree (*tous azimuths*) deterrence posture that would assume no one external enemy.

Kokoshin spotlighted emergent thinking in an interview with *Krasnaya Zvezda* in March 1992.[217] He first noted the abiding fundamental: the development of *doctrine* must be a joint civilian-military undertaking. He underlined the fact of profound, continuing socio-economic crisis; the 'war' between Whites and Reds must end. Finally, he focused on military prescription. He called for 'high technology' Air Force, Strategic Rocket Forces and Navy (coastal forces complementing air and land forces, plus strategic missile carriers in the Barents and Okhotsk Seas), and 'small but efficient general purpose forces'--centrally based rapid deployment forces. Their strategic reserve core would be 'several airmobile brigades', with their own army aviation, fire support, electronic warfare, intelligence and counter optico-electronic systems.[218] Kokoshin's prescription echoed the *Afghantsy* agenda: high technology; focus on the potency and prospects of new and evolving technologies; and emphasis on *spetsnaz* and special forces on the ground.

---

[215] G. Schoenfeld, 'Troops or Consequences', *Post-Soviet Prospects*, CSIS 21 (September 1993).

[216] *Moscow Radio* (all-Union), 19 November 1991.

[217] *Krasnaya Zvezda*, 17 March 1992.

[218] *Kuranti*, 15 April 1992; see also Kipp, *European Security*, 233.

Russia's new military was significantly leaner.[219] Yet it was determined to maintain quality, local and regional interventionary capacity and global strike potential: 'Russia's Armed Forces must be able to wage warfare of any character or kind and on any scale.'[220]

The new military leadership was forged in and by the war in Afghanistan. This made it particularly sensitive to the problems and difficulties of counterinsurgency campaigns and needs. It instilled and reinforced bias favouring 'smart' weaponry and elite units. Finally, it sharpened patriotism and pride--and appreciation of the dangers of dogma. The *Afghantsy* succeeded in Afghanistan; they left a government in control of every city, base and major artery. Their government ordained withdrawal for political and foreign policy, not military reasons. The *Afghantsy* took pride in the fact that their withdrawal was *not* like that of US forces from Vietnam.

In the wake of the failed August 1991 coup the KGB had been reduced from 490,000 men to 35-40,000, as its military and counter-intelligence units (together with most special forces Interior Ministry troops), were transferred to the army.[221] The association was accepted but dreaded by the army, for it eliminated the threshold that protected it from early and necessary involvement in civil conflict. The return of these units and troops to the Security Ministry (which the Law on Security of May and the Law on Federal Organs of State Security of June 1992 established as KGB successor, together with the now separated Foreign Intelligence Service)[222] thus reestablished the State's internal security option, sought by Yeltsin, while allowing the army to distance itself--which would stand it in good stead during the October days of 1993.

Civilian control was not questioned--though, as suggested by the discussion of Russian strategic culture, above, the word control is to some extent deceptive. The Russian parliament established successor oversight committees to those of the now defunct Supreme Soviet. The party watchdog Military Political Administration was abolished, replaced by a

---

[219] The navy's 60 per cent reduction in submarine procurement rates in 1991 was symptomatic, as was its more rapid retirement of older vessels (in the Pacific 29 older nuclear submarines were retired in 1989-90 and another 29 in 1991, leaving 40 newer models); *Jane's Defence Weekly*, 5 October 1991.

[220] Colonel General Rodionov, 'Some Approaches to Elaboration of Russia's Military Doctrine', *Voennaya Mysl* (special issue), July 1992.

[221] See *Le Monde*, 15 October 1991, and *New York Times*, 10 November 1991.

[222] See also A. Rahr, 'The Revival of a Strong KGB', *RFE/RL Research Report*, 14 May 1993; and V. Yasman, 'Where Has the KGB Gone?', *RFE/RL Research Report*, 8 January 1993.

president-appointed and parliament-sanctioned Higher Certification Commission 'responsible for overseeing personnel questions within the new Defence Ministry'.[223]

A new, more conservative centre-right consensus appeared to have emerged. The days of the most sweeping reform and 'democracy' advocacies and debates were over. The Higher Certification Commission was chaired by Yurii Skokov, an ally also of Rutskoi, Khazbulatov and the 'industrialists' lobby', and Secretary of the Russian Security Council—which was given increased powers by Yeltsin in July 1992.[224]

The consensus was best summarized by *The Strategy for Russia*, produced by the Council for Foreign and Defence Policy in August 1992. The Council 'unites politicians, businessmen, civilian analysts and journalists of what is usually described as the liberal outlook... [it represents] the most sophisticated trend of the mainstream democratic opinion which would be happy to have a democracy in Russia but ready and willing to admit the necessity of an authoritarian rule and enhancing of statism [*gosudarstvennost*]'.[225] Vladimir Lukin (who may have been among *The Strategy for Russia*'s authors) characterized its message as 'enlightened patriotism'.[226]

*

From order undermined to Yeltsin coup and consequences. The apparent new order of autumn 1992 soon dissipated, however, amidst evermore rancorous breakdown of relations between Yeltsin and parliamentary leaders--erstwhile Yeltsin allies who now turned against the presidency. The end of 1992 and early 1993 saw a 'war of decrees' whereby each institution sought to negate the other's initiatives and promote its own agenda. In March Yeltsin tried to impose special rule, but failed when Army and Security Ministers opposed extralegal action, by president or parliament.

---

[223] Foye, 'Post Soviet Russia'.

[224] *Izvestia*, 10 July 1992; see also *RFE/RL Research Report*, 8 May 1992, for a background report on the 'industrialists' lobby'; and *New York Times*, 25 October 1992 for a profile on Khazbulatov.

[225] 'The Strategy for Russia: Some Theses for The Council for Foreign and Defence Policy's Report', *Nezavisimaya Gazeta*, 19 August 1992. Quotes from A.A. Kalinin (Member, Defence Committee of the Moscow City Council), 'On the Meaning and Preliminary Results of the Recent Debates in Defence and Security Issues in the Late USSR and New Democratic Russia', unpublished manuscript October 1992, available from author.

[226] V. Lukin, 'Our Security Predicament', *Foreign Policy* (Fall 1992), 66.

Yeltsin fired Security Minister Barannikov (as he had his reformist predecessor--who now supported Barannikov) and the Security Council's Skokov, who was equally critical.[227] He barely escaped impeachment. The decreed referendums decreed by Yeltsin that followed, on 25 April, revived his authority; majorities confirmed confidence, supported his economic programme, and called for early parliamentary elections. Yet they showed a certain precariousness of support. The question of early presidential elections, which Yeltsin opposed, was rejected by only 49.8 to 49.1 per cent, notwithstanding the government's dominance of TV and media; nearly 40 per cent abstained.[228] Parliament disdained the results. Yeltsin's smearing of opponents as communists and fascists elicited scorn--and reverse character assassination. The war of decrees continued, amidst growing public disenchantment with both institutions.

Refusing to accept the parliamentary supremacy that was fundamental to the now (after more than 300 amendments) post-Soviet constitution, Yeltsin tried through the spring to negotiate a strong presidency constitution with regional leaders. The procedure was unconstitutional, and entailed a certain burning of the bridges to parliament. This in turn gave regional leaders inordinate leverage, which they used to extract fiscal and other powers that ultimately made a mockery of Yeltsin's purpose. To submit this 'constitution' to a referendum (as initially promised) would have eviscerated his power even more than would submission to parliament.

By early summer, notwithstanding instances of often petty rancour (Yeltsin reacted to Rutskoi's criticism by depriving him of car and privileges--much as he had previously done to Gorbachev), there were signs of possible reconciliation. Khazbulatov defended Shaposhnikov, Yeltsin's choice as new Security Council Secretary, against attacks from conservative/nationalist parliamentarians. Yeltsin overrode radical calls for the ouster of centrist Prime Minister Victor Chernomyrdin for the latter's proclamation of a currency reform that undercut savings and neighbour-state finances. The reform's consequent effect of strengthening successor state leaders who sought influence within a collegial tent (and return to a rouble zone), rather than estrangement and uncertainty without, strengthened moderate power and prospects for compromise.

Yet the principal differences, over presidential powers and economic prescription, as also the psychological residue of loyalties lost and 'betrayed', remained unresolved--together with the related issue of Yeltsin's preference for rule by decree (evident even when the parliamentary majority was sympathetic, as when it elected him, and later his designated

---

[227] *RFE/RL Research Report,* 14 May 1993.

[228] *Economist,* 1 May 1993.

94

successor, as its speaker). Yeltsin's opponents, crucial to the defence of democracy in August 1991, were of course not the communists of later propaganda. They had no wish to return to the oppressive and corrupt system bequeathed by Brezhnev (which also, incidentally, had about as much to do with communist ideals as Pinochet's Chilean dictatorship had to do with Plato). No military or industrial leader wanted to return to the days when decisions were made by bureaucrats in Moscow. But they equated Yeltsin's Big Bang privatization programme with laundering and legalizing of the mafia's and the old *apparat*'s ill-gotten gains, with the further enriching of these groups, and also foreign interests, through bargain basement sell-off of Russian assets (who but they had the money to buy?), and, in general, with throwing the baby out with the bathwater in terms of national and moral values.

Yeltsin's opponents did not want to return to the old. Rather, they looked to Japan and the Asian tigers, and the prescription for German and French economic success, namely state-private planning and coordination. Allied industrial managers might ask for subsidies to avert bankruptcy. But their goal was to become themselves multinationals, players on the global scene--not to resubmit to 'command economy' management.

They had no wish to return to East-West confrontation. They supported cooperation with Washington on most issues. They favoured the UN and peacekeeping, but also more vigorous pursuit of what they deemed intrinsic Russian interests. They were dubious about sanctions against Serbia and Iraq, which they saw as counterproductive to their ostensible and original purpose. And they advocated greater attention to Asia and the Pacific Rim.

Yet gridlock continued (though, as will be seen, propelled ever more by personal rather than policy disputes), with its corollaries of increasing economic and political anarchy, increased public disenchantment with due process, and increased elite concern and impatience. The latter centred on two issues. Ukraine's spring-summer 1993 descent into hyperinflation underlined the urgency of economic reform, and the dangers of money-printing palliatives. At the same time the backdrop of civil wars along the periphery of the old Union underlined the dangers that attended centrifugal tendencies within Russia as well.

Yeltsin's and parliament's wooing of the armed forces became more assiduous. Yeltsin's sweeping list of summer promotions was preemptive and decisive; it brought Rutskoi's final, irrevocable break with the presidency. He noted that Russia's far smaller forces now had more generals than the Soviet mastodon, charged Yeltsin with buying off rather than reforming, and castigated both Yeltsin and the army leadership as innately corrupt.[229] The charge was exaggerated; generals dismissed far outnumbered generals

---

[229] *Rossiskaya Gazeta*, 17 June 1993.

added.[230] In light of later events it may also have been fatal. Its indiscriminate sweep alienated the *Afghantsy* reformers, his most natural army constituency.

The Yeltsin coup that followed was well prepared; by August 'The edict [to dismiss parliament] lay in my safe and waited for its time to come'.[231] The run-up provoked fundamental change in political constellations and parameters. The apparent new order of mid and late 1992 had rested on compromise between Yeltsinite fast reform advocates and the slow reform/social compact programme of the Civic Union; the departure of Acting Premier Yegor Gaidar, architect of the fast reform blueprint, and his replacement by Viktor Chernomyrdin, a Civic Union associate, though with Gaidar allies retaining core portfolios, was seen to herald the new compromise course. With the formula's implementation stymied by political gridlock, however, and ever more concerned by inflation and the Ukrainian example, Chernomyrdin himself and a growing subsection of the Civic Union constituency became persuaded that monetary discipline and faster reform were essential. Gaidar's return as Deputy Prime Minister in September 1993 signalled acceptance by Chernomyrdin and others of the need for a more radical approach.

The other element of the new consensus focused on the need to reverse now galloping centrifugal dynamics. Yeltsin's 1992 acceptance of the army's nationalist agenda on the Kuriles and Moldova, and of its self-proclaimed guardianship of the Russian diaspora, had appeared resigned rather than supportive. By summer 1993, however, Yeltsin took the lead in hoisting the Russia First banner. In the process, his courtship of the army (see also below), which may initially have been viewed as little more than tactical insurance to safeguard position and policy, became integral to the definition both of a markedly different personal status and a markedly different policy.

Yeltsin welcomed the attendant/intended consequence of Chernomyrdin's currency reform. The initially sparked reintegration of successor states within the rouble zone was reversed when it became clear that Moscow's monopoly control of fiscal and monetary policy would eviscerate their sovereignty. The potentially centrifugal ramifications of the reversal were negated by larger dynamics. Regional conflicts and fears, finely calibrated by Moscow, compelled Central Asian and Caucasian support for Russian peacekeeping, and CIS entry by previously recalcitrant Georgia and Azerbaijan. The end result was Russian security dominance, without the concomitant of societal and economic obligation (an emergent analogue to US-Central American relations?).

---

[230] *Nezavisimaya Gazeta*, 7 July 1993.

[231] German *ARD TV* interview with Yeltsin, 12 November 1993.

Yeltsin also welcomed Chernomyrdin's role in securing expanded rights for Ukraine's Russian population, through the negotiations at the end of June that followed the Donbass strikes.[232] He condemned Estonia's anti-Russian citizenship law (a sharp letter to the UN Secretary General referred to 'ethnic cleansing'), and encouraged subsequent autonomy votes by Narva and other Russian enclaves. Where Shaposhnikov as CIS Defence Minister had previously asserted CIS' sole authority to conduct peacekeeping and peacemaking within the borders of the former USSR, Yeltsin now (the CIS post was folded into Russia's Ministry in May)[233] dispatched his Foreign Minister to assert Russia's successor claim, and press for UN funding.[234]

Yeltsin's determined courtship of the army, which began after Skokov's resignation, extended also to Security and Interior Ministries and troops. Weekly and often more frequent meetings with Defence Minister Grachev placed the latter among Yeltsin's most intimate advisors. The army received disproportionate funding increases, and (as noted) an increasingly positive presidential embrace of its domestic and 'Near Abroad' agenda. Shaposhnikov's later resignation from the Security Council secretaryship (because of limited access to Yeltsin) confirmed the fact that much of its role and function was now subsumed within the new direct relationship between Yeltsin and Grachev. The independence accorded the army leadership was also reflected in Kokoshin's Defence protocol slip from second to third, behind the Chief of the General Staff.

Finally, Yeltsin's nationalist credentials were signally reinforced by his meeting with Ukraine's President Kravchuk a few weeks before the coup--when he threatened to cut off energy exports if past bills were not paid. Kravchuk agreed in principle to transfer Ukrainian assets in lieu of payments due. Assets specified included strategic nuclear forces and the 50 per cent of the Black Sea Fleet that their previous June meeting had destined for Ukrainian ownership (sparking army protest).[235] Initial Russian reports presented a *fait accompli*, a garnishing of a delinquent's assets. Ukrainian transcripts, and subsequent Russian

---

[232] For Ukrainian coverage, see *Golos Ukrainy*, 29 June 1993, p 1.

[233] See *International Herald Tribune*, 16 June 1993; the Supreme Command of the Commonwealth Joint Armed forces would be replaced by a 'united headquarters for coordinating military cooperation'.

[234] See, for example, *Economist*, 28 August and 18 September 1993; also *RFE/RL Research Report*, 9 April 1993, for background; and *ITAR-TASS*, 1 March 1993, for Yeltsin's first embrace of this posture: 'the time has come for...the United Nations to grant Russia special powers as guarantor of peace and stability in this region.'

[235] See, for example, Fred Hiatt, 'Economic Disaster Speeds Ukraine Pact', *Guardian Weekly*, 12 September 1993.

government pronouncements, were more circumspect. Kiev insisted particularly that mobile SS-24 missiles were excluded, and that the deal in any case represented no more than a yet-to-be-negotiated possibility.[236] Nevertheless, in the context of Ukraine's debt and bankruptcy, the agreement in principle charted a resolution of nuclear and fleet frictions that satisfied Russian nationalist demands, in a way that also assuaged at least some Ukrainian sensibilities. (Its nuclear provisions were effectively confirmed in January 1994, when Ukraine's parliament ratified Kravchuk's acceptance that *all* missiles would be transferred to Russia within three years.)[237]

The September coup, when it came, thus succeeded because of elite impatience with the ramifications and dangers of continued *status quo*, because of impatience with democratic niceties and widespread public apathy, and (perhaps most startlingly) because Yeltsin coopted core segments of his opponents' constituencies.

The coup freed Yeltsin from the tedium of legality. His dismissal of constitution and parliament was followed (after the carnage at the Ostankino TV building, when Internal Security troops fired on the pro-parliament mob that tried to storm it, and the bloody assault on parliament) by dismissal of the Constitutional, or Supreme Court, all elected republic and district assemblies, and finally also municipal governments, the country's last elected bodies. Khazbulatov, Rutskoi and other parliamentary leaders and supporters were jailed. The formal censorship imposed with the coup was lifted, but only after the banning of opposition parties and newspapers. Yeltsin's apparent authority was as absolute as any tsar's; his cavalier dismissal on 6 November of presidential elections promised for June 1994 reinforced the notion. (The promise, made during the crisis days of parliamentary defiance, may always have been tactical rather than strategic, goading parliament--which insisted on simultaneous parliamentary and presidential elections in February--into the scripted denouement.)[238]

But the appearance of total control was illusory. Yeltsin was beholden to the *boyars* [noblemen] who secured his victory, committed to core elements of their agendas, and dependent on them for policy implementation. His post-coup strong and, some would say, imperial presidency constitution (which also eliminated secession rights) proceeded towards referendum judgement coincident with decreed *Duma* (parliament's pre-1917 name)

---

[236] Ukraine's obfuscation brought Russian Foreign Minister Kozyrev's assertion on 7 December that 'Sevastopol had always been a Russian naval base and would remain so...the Massandra agreements providing for Ukraine to hand over the fleet to Russia in Exchange for debt relief (must) be honoured...Russia would 'not allow' another nuclear state on its border'; *Interfax*, as reported in *RFE/RL Daily Report*, 8 December 1993.

[237] See, for example, *Guardian Weekly*, 6 February 1994.

[238] Jonathan Steele (*Guardian* Moscow correspondent), 'Yeltsin's Conspiracy; Evidence suggests Russian leader set Parliament up for a fall', *Ottawa Citizen* et al., 29 November 1993.

December elections, themselves legitimized only by the presumption of constitutional passage. Yet the limits to his personal authority soon became evident. Yeltsin was forced to reverse his ban on opposition parties and papers, though jailed parliamentary leaders were not allowed to stand for election, and to rescind his dismissal of early presidential elections.[239] Core reform allies decried the 'dictatorial' prescription of the submitted constitution, and insisted that, even if passed, it must be amended.[240]

Yeltsin retained control of national television. Favouritism was blatant: the Gaidar-led Russia's Choice pro-Yeltsin 'shock therapy' reform party was given ten times the exposure of any other; during the first 12 days of the campaign Gaidar was given 144 times more air time than Grigory Yavlinsky, leader of the dissident reform Yavlinsky-Boldyrev-Lukin, or Yabloko bloc. (Lukin resigned his Washington ambassadorship in the runup to Yeltsin's September coup.)[241] In fact, the void left by Rutskoi's incarceration had been filled: even a post-election pro-reform majority, if it could be assembled, would clearly be closer to Rutskoi's prescription than to Yeltsin's. Any consequent pro-reform government would perforce demand amendments similar to those championed by Rutskoi.

The ultimate irony, perhaps, was the fact that constitutional passage (during the campaign the 'goalposts' moved in response to polls suggesting widespread apathy, from necessary approval by a majority of voters to approval by 50 per cent plus one of a voting minimum of just half of the electorate) would be secured by voters who otherwise supported communist/nationalist and conservative anti-Yeltsin parties. On election day, 12 December, a CNN exit poll suggested only 37 per cent would have supported Yeltsin for president; Yeltsin's office announced he would avail himself of the new constitution's provision that he serve out his original term--there would be no early presidential election.[242]

By January 1994, after the first sessions of the new *Duma*, it was clear that the faster reform consensus was no longer sustainable. Yeltsin embraced Chernomyrdin's move back to the slower reform prescription of late 1992; Gaidar again left the government, as did its other 'monetarist' champion, Finance Minister Boris Fedorov.[243] Shock therapy might or might not be economically optimal; it was clearly not politically viable. The new-old

---

[239] Yeltsin interview, 15 November 1993, *Izvestia.*

[240] *Interfax*; *RFE/RL Daily Report,* 6 December 1993.

[241] *RFE/RL Daily Report*, 26 November 1993; *ITAR-TASS*, 2 December 1993.

[242] *CNN*, 12 December 1993.

[243] For example, *New York Times*, 27 January 1994.

prescription was essentially Gorbachevian and Rutskoian; its defining Russia First (and Larger Russia) parameters were quintessentially Rutskoian.

Aggrandized by an apparently aggrandized presidency, Yeltsin was diminished, for he could scarcely smear 'his' parliament as he had smeared its predecessor. His new parliamentary dismissal prerogative was emasculated by the likelihood that its early exercise would result in even harsher voter backlash. He was, in fact, more beholden than before.

On 30 January the *Duma* elections were played out again in Crimea. A Russian secessionist swept to the presidency, crushing his pro-Kiev opponent--and hostile media coverage.[244] Sentiment in Eastern Ukraine (promised a spring poll) had followed a parallel momentum since the summer strikes. Theirs were Russian and Russified populations that clearly fell within the Yeltsin-sanctioned 'protection' mandate of Russia's new defence doctrine (see also below).

*

Arms and society: course set? Of the *boyars* who secured Yeltsin's victory, none was more important than the army, the final arbiter of the 3-4 October showdown, and now the country's only real arbiter. And it emerged thus in a context that was unique to Russian history. Through tsarist and Soviet times it had as previously described been integrated into larger composite leaderships, through ties of organization and family. Now the party which had defined that integration for nearly three-quarters of a century was gone. The successor structure of elected legislative authority and oversight bodies was an early casualty of the war of decrees, succeeded only by the personal conclaves between Yeltsin and Minister (and Defence Collegium; see below). The presidency as primary oversight authority was integral to the December 1993 constitution. Yet Yeltsin commanded neither the administrative nor political cadres needed to effect new integrative and supervisory structures.

More extraordinary still, the army's unprecedented authority and independence was achieved through only minimal exposure to and responsibility for the coup's bloody denouement. Indeed, the army's official posture had been one of institutional 'neutrality' (as was that of the church). It was a posture dictated by the absolute concern to maintain army unity; Rutskoi still had supporters. Grachev provided decisive personal support to Yeltsin. And the army's neutrality was clearly benevolent to Yeltsin's course, in that it did not take contrary action. But the troops involved in the eye-to-eye carnage at Ostankino and the White House were of the Ministries of the Interior and Security--the limited and select

---

[244] *Nezavizimaya Gazeta, Independent*, and *New York Times,* 31 January 1994.

support provided by the army was decisive, yet it was at one remove.[245] The army as such was remarkably untainted. Thus it not only emerged as the ultimate arbiter of the nation's fate; it did so with a surprisingly strong claim to non-partisanship.

That claim was further strengthened by post-coup suggestions, first by Yeltsin aide (General) Dmitrii Volkogonov and later by Yeltsin himself, that Grachev had in fact been reluctant to intervene against parliament--perhaps out of 'fear that others in the military leadership would not stand behind him...in the event, according to Yeltsin, the military leadership as a whole proved more reliable than the Defence Minister'.[246] Since Grachev was not asked to resign, and did not, one might surmise that the suggestions were in fact designed to 'de-taint' him. But if that was their purpose, their consequence clearly reinforced the image and reality of non-partisanship.

The worst case Latin-Americanization suggested by pre-coup socio-economic dynamics and the attendant post-coup possibility of caesarism was perhaps a less likely scenario. On the one hand, the socio-economic understanding that secured sufficient centre support for the coup to proceed was sympathetic to Yeltsin's fast reform agenda, yet did also assuage the centre's primary concerns. On the other hand, the army clearly remained preoccupied by the continuing problems of transition and transformation, and focused on the task of modernization.[247] Its officer corps, freed from the ties that bound them to society, remained bound to the culture that decreed such ties.

Yeltsin was clearly beholden, and acknowledged this in his post-coup declaration of immediate priority to the task of ratifying the new defence doctrine. The gap between Yeltsin promises (including a coup-timed doubling of officer salaries) and actual government largesse would be bridged.[248] Yet military leaders were fully cognizant of economic realities --the backlog of housing and social costs associated with still continuing withdrawal from Germany and contraction dynamics, wage pressure and the pressure of the lure of alternative

---

[245] Tanks and soldiers from the elite Taman and Kantemirovsky Divisions and airborne forces from Tula gave decisive support; see Fred Hiatt 'Neither Russia nor its army are likely to ever be the same', *Washington Post*, 5 October 1993. But the troops inside the Ostankino building that opened fire on the pro-Parliament mob that attempted to seize control were *Omon*; the commandos who stormed (into) Parliament were *Alpha*.

[246] *RFE/RL Daily Report*, 15 November 1993; German *ARD TV*, 12 November 1993.

[247] See especially J.W.R. Lepingwell, 'Is the Military Disintegrating?', *RFE/RL Research Report*, 18 June 1993.

[248] In mid-August government payments were two trillion roubles in arrears; See Schoenfeld, 'Troops or Consequences'.

employment on the leadership's determination to save and develop high technology potential.[249]

This led to acceptance of prospects for an even smaller armed forces structure, but with concomitant stress on higher quality. This in turn meant higher quality draftees (increasingly unlikely, in view of draft dodging's social acceptability) or faster conversion to all volunteer troops. The latter proceeded, and accelerated--in part because of the success of an appeal for female applicants, drawn not just to the medical services, but also to non-traditional areas such as air defence (causing some male backlash).[250] By summer 1993, Grachev was foreseeing an all volunteer elite force of just one million.[251] The conscription umbilical cord to society at large was severed.

The new doctrine, when formalized, mirrored 1992's draft: *tous azimuths* preparedness; threats against the rights and interests of Russians in the near abroad were explicitly listed as warranting army response, as were outside efforts to interfere in Russia's internal affairs and attacks on Russian military installations on foreign territory; first use of nuclear weapons was sanctioned against nuclear weapon states (this clause, which mirrored longstanding NATO policy, was also a wake-up call to Kiev); offensive operations were given a formal green light; the restriction on armed forces manning was rescinded.[252] *Afghantsys'* priorities had received across the board approval, plus markers for a less financially strapped future (see below).

Meanwhile, socio-economic circumstance also accelerated the army's move away from past divisional and service structures. Armies and divisions would be replaced by corps and brigades (thus concluding one debate). Old service divisions would be transcended. 'Joint Commands' were created in the Far East and the now amalgamated Siberian and Transbaikal Military Districts, with their commanders given deputy minister status and more independence--signalling a move away from the strict central control of past tradition and practice. Grachev had heralded the change in January, when he called for revamping old MD structures:

Instead... it would be advisable to set up four to six armed forces with geographic designation (for example Western, Central, North Caucasus, Volga-Ural, Siberian

[249] *Krasnaya Zvezda*, 20 March 1993.

[250] *Ibid.*, 30 January and 10 April 1993; see also *Voenno-ekonomichesky zhurnal*, #3 1993.

[251] *ITAR-TASS*, 7 May 1993.

[252] *Kommersant Daily*, 17 November 1993; *Izvestia*, 18 November 1993.

and Far Eastern strategic commands)... military districts that exist... could be transformed into mobilization districts.[253]

The North Caucasus received priority attention, reflecting the *Afghantsys'* primary threat spectrums--against, through or from Russia's Caucasian and South Central Asian underbelly.[254] Also integrating Cossack formations, border troops and Interior Ministry units, it was strengthened by an airborne division, two airborne and three motorized rifle brigades, air transport and combat forces, and parts of the old Nineteenth Independent Air Defence Army.[255]

A new service equivalent Mobile Forces Command integrated aeromobile, air mobile potential and related forces, and high readiness ground components; it was subdivided into an immediate reaction force, with parts destined for North Caucasus service, and a somewhat 'heavier' rapid deployment force.[256] To this was added a specially designated elite peacekeeping division, with a regiment in Moldova, and a battalion in Ossetia.[257]

Traditionalists like Ground Forces Commander Vladimir Semenov opposed the 'bleeding dry of the other services and branches of the armed forces', and argued the continuing relevance of older structures and combined operations concepts.[258] But the *Afghantsys'* more decentralized, more flexible, more mobile and higher technology prescription for future war prevailed.

The prescription dictated maintenance of military research and development, increased 'smart' weapons production and more sophisticated command, control, communications and intelligence systems.[259]

The prescription's primary immediate concern, to combat southern threats--that is, fundamentalist Islam--also cemented much improved relations with China. Beijing's concerns about Islamic resurgence in Sinkiang led to vigorous support for a Russian posture that would protect and secure a secular buffer. Russian-Chinese military cooperation,

---

[253] *Rossiiskie Vesti*, 4 January 1993.

[254] *Nezavisimaya Gazeta*, 7 May 1993.

[255] *Krasnaya Zvezda*, 18 March 1993; *Segodnya*, 10 March 1993; *RFE/RL Research Report*, 18 June 1993.

[256] *Krasnaya Zvezda*, 18 December 1992, presents peacetime and wartime organizational structures; see also *Krasnaya Zvezda*, 6 May 1993.

[257] *Krasnaya Zvezda*, 7, 12 May 1993.

[258] *Ibid.*, 18 December 1992 and 28 April 1993.

[259] *Nezavisimaya Gazeta*, 3 June 1993.

signalled also by a rapidly expanding Chinese market for Russian arms exports and joint development ventures, was summarized most startlingly by the signing of a five–year military cooperation agreement, and Grachev's commentary on 11 November that 'the two countries hoped to restore the close ties that had once united the Soviet Union and China' (though a formal alliance was not envisioned).[260]

The army's Near Abroad agenda was in fact remarkably successful. The Moldovan intervention model of 1992 (surgical intervention, direct or indirect, to check anti-Russian dynamics and establish pro-Russian players, with generally arms-length follow-up limited to that needed to perpetuate a now more dependent *status quo*) was repeated successfully through the southern conflict regions. In Tajikistan Russian forces provided just sufficient logistic and special forces aid to defeat the insurrectionist democratic-Islamicist government, then limited subsequent involvement to sealing the Tajik/Afghan border; after Abkhazia was given sufficient support to deny Georgian control, Russian 'protection' of rail lines and port facilities saved Tbilisi from defeat at the hands of ex-President Gamsakhurdia's rebels, and brought Georgia into the CIS; concomitantly, Moscow's successful, preemptive denial to Turkish and Iranian intervention suggestions, combined with continuing Armenian Nagorno-Karabakh military success (with ex-Soviet arms and at least some covert Russian support) and Turkish military instructors' failure to turn the tide, brought Azerbaijan also into the CIS--the price for Russian aid sufficient to blunt, though not (yet) reverse Armenian gain.[261] The principle of a Russian security zone, though without empire's attendant costs of social and political responsibility, was established. Whether the low cost 'Central Americanization' formula could be perpetuated was another matter; the sophisticated *realpolitik* balancing that bought it would need constant attending, and that in turn would require a consistency of purpose and a degree of socio-economic home stability that could not be presumed.

The Russian state's pre- and post-coup acceptance of the *Afghantsys*' prescription, the now positive procurement trend and new funding prospects augured well for continuing army transformation and reform.[262] But the question of a new, viable social compact is clearly tied to still uncertain prospects for stability and legitimacy posited by both late 1993 and 1995 Duma elections, and to the socio–economic success of the new/old economic

---

[260] *RFE/RL Research Report*, 12 November 1993; on the military cooperation agreement, see also *ITAR-TASS*, 9 November 1993.

[261] *RFL/RL Research Report*, 9 April 1993; *ITAR-TASS*, 11 November 1993; the *Ottawa Citizen*, 23 November 1993; see also coverage of doctrine, above.

[262] See for example 'Privileges promised to the defence industry', *Moscow News*, 2 July 1993; and *ITAR-TASS*, 25 November 1993.

reform prescription. If state structures fail to support and finance, the spectre of *caesarism* (and the *Freikorps* implications of independent, extralegal funding) may find new converts.

*

Yeltsin's inglorious Chechnya campaign--Army failure or reaffirmation?--; ramifications for the future. The Yeltsin government's assault early in 1995 on Grosny and on Dzhokhat Dudayev's separatist government, brought media images of military insubordination, bungling and incompetence, civilians caught in the crossfire, and near-wanton destruction. Western and some Russian commentary saw military ineptness and crudity, low morale, poor doctrine and a return to authoritarianism. Others decried any use of force, though their own countries had often used (sometimes excessive) force against insurgencies. Muslim leaders saw assault against Islam, though Dudayev's embrace of the faith was as opportunistic and incongruent as Saddam Hussein's a few years earlier. Yet in the end the events may have positive rather than negative consequences in Moscow--though Chechen alienation will no doubt fester.

The most startling point about the offensive, coordinated by Defence Minister Pavel Grachev and the other security ministers, was that the elite of the Russian army was not involved. Its most popular and respected commanders--including, most notably, Deputy Defence Minister Boris Gromov and the Fourteenth Army's General Alexander Lebed--publicly condemned the campaign, refused to participate, and refused to allow their troops to be dispatched. The elite Ekaterinburg Interior Ministry unit involved in the initial assault soon packed their bags and flew home. Of the three assault columns assembled from what could be assembled, from the army (mostly raw recruits), Interior Ministry troops and border guards, the commanders of two refused to attack 'civilian targets'--one stopping in a glare of publicity, the other halting his advance without fanfare. Gromov described the action as 'barbaric' and 'unnecessary' (reflecting the prevailing opinion that isolation, internal opposition and covert aid could have ended Chechnya's secession) and unnecessarily alienating. To use the army for domestic suppression was in any case 'unconstitutional'; such operations were the responsibility of the Ministry of the Interior, and the police. Lebed was equally scathing: the campaign made a martyr of a criminal and popularized a dwindling insurrection; worse, the incompetence of its launch and prosecution reminded him of Finland in 1940, when 'troops went in to take the wool off the sheep and came out sheared themselves'.[263]

---

[263] Lebed, in interview to *Radio Echo* (Moscow), 8 January 1995; see also Steven Erlanger, 'Russian military shows signs of deep crisis', *New York Times*, 23 December 1994; Alessandra Stanley, 'The shadowy

The mutinies of high and lower command occasioned no arrest, no court-martial. Reports in mid-January asserted the dismissal of six generals, yet none left their post; reports at the end of January of the dismissal of Gromov and others also brought no change. The reformers' darkest fear appeared to be unfolding. Startlingly, however, there was no panic. The mutineers were protected by near unanimous armed forces support. But they were also protected by overwhelming popular support, and near unanimous political support from reformers and traditionalists, from democrats, communists and nationalists alike (except Vladimir Zhirinovsky's neo-fascists, who supported Yeltsin). A *Duma* vote confirmed Interior Ministry responsibility for Chechnya. Yeltsin agreed; he had little choice. New rumours spoke of Grachev as scapegoat.

A 'dirty little' war would continue to simmer in the Caucasus, but it had occasioned no split in the army. It had, to the contrary, confirmed extraordinary unity among its best and brightest. And though the unity was in opposition to an elected president, it rested on constitutional principle--a principle supported by the legislature and, later, however reluctantly, by the executive. Yeltsin was isolated and, in the eyes of most, discredited, yet he was not removed. The army would support the constitution, not undermine it. Lebed professed admiration for Pinochet's Chilean development model, but decried extremist policies ('truth always lies in the middle'). It now appeared probable that if there was to be a military commander-in-chief in Russia's future, it would follow the Eisenhower precedent of service retirement and ballot victory.

Finally, Lebed's 1995 analogy had an unspoken corollary. In 1940 the mismanagement and excessive casualties of the Winter War against Finland discredited Marshals Kliment Voroshilov and Semyon Budenny, who had inherited army leadership after Stalin's military purges of 1937 gutted the high command. Marshal Georgi Zhukov, who had defeated the Japanese at Lake Khazan and Khalkin Gol (in 1938 and 1939), was recalled, and the process of renewal that ultimately led to the Wehrmacht and Nazi defeat was begun. In Grosny, again, conflict mismanagement discredited a Defence Minister who owed his position to personalized political loyalty. And, again, the catharsis paved the way for more independent, professional leadership. As a result, prospects for thorough military reform untainted by corruption have clearly improved. So also, therefore, are prospects for a constitutional, reformed Russia.

The first step towards renewal may have been taken with the surprise announcement early in February that General Gromov would assume the position of 'chief military expert'

---

man at Yeltsin's side', *New York Times*, 7 January 1995; Erlanger, 'Chechens, Russians dig in for guerilla war', *New York Times*, 17 January; and Tony Barber, 'Elite Russian unit mutinies', *The Independent*, 4 February 1995.

in the Foreign Ministry, responsible for 'overseeing military cooperation within the Commonwealth of Independent States'.[264] The new position, effectively Coordinator in Chief for the Armed Forces of the CIS, reflected evolving acceptance of the concept of common security space; it also entailed some authority vis-à-vis Russia's own armed forces and Defence Ministry.

A second, indirect step might be identified in General Lebed's resignation from the army in June 1995, with the words 'the president is sick and tired of me and I am sick and tired of him'.[265] Lebed joined the centrist Congress of Russian Communities, and surged to the top of opinion polls gauging prospects for the 1996 Presidential election--with double Yeltsin's support. The coincidence of an independent (still undeclared) former military General, Colin Powell, heading similar US pre-Presidential election polls was noteworthy.[266]

A Lebed victory and its likely import remained speculative; Grigory Yavlinsky was a close second in the polls. But disenchantment with Yeltsin was manifest. And Chernomyrdin's alternative candidacy, suggested by his launch of the Yeltsin-allied 'Our Home is Russia' party, his peaceful stealing-the-limelight resolution of the Budennovsk [Chechen] hostage crisis and subsequent negotiations towards a resolution of the war in Chechnya, lost credibility with the defeat of a prominent ally in elections for the Sverdlovsk regional government, and unrefuted charges of corruption and illegal profiteering from energy industry privatization; similar charges again smeared Defence Minister Grachev, while privatization impresario Chubais, though not personally accused of corruption, was charged with 'fire sale of Russian resources' to foreigners and the less reputable.[267]

Lebed's embrace of larger-union nostalgia under the Russia First banner, strong central authority and unremitting anti-corruption determination certainly corresponded to late 1995 majority will--more so than Yavlinsky's more moderate formulations. Yet Lebed's embrace also of a government-committed social agenda, one aspect of which was suggested by early support for the Green Party, also echoed Powell's coalition formula of patriotism with social conscience. Whether to be pursued through a Lebed presidency or that of another, repositioned candidate's, it was a winning formula, representative of spreading consensus.

---

[264] 'Russia agrees to partial Chechnya truce', *Southam News Service*, 14 February 1995.

[265] The *International Herald Tribune*, 15 June 1995.

[266] See 'Europe. A man to watch', *The Economist*, 7 October 1995; and Alessandra Stanley, 'General woos disenchanted voters', *New York Times*, 14 October 1995.

[267] See Peter Reddaway, 'Is Chernomyrdin A Crook?', *Post-Soviet Prospects*, CSIS, Washington, August 1995; also *Izvestia*, 21 March 1995, and *Obshchaya Gazeta*, 29 June 1995.

In the South it reinforced the momentum of previous decisions, through assertive further build-up of southern/Caucasian force structures, and **de facto** Western agreement that contrary CFE Treaty restrictions on 'Flank' numbers would not be enforced.[268] The assertiveness was reflected also in more determined policies towards Bosnia/Yugoslavia and other conflicts and arenas.

The late 1995 consensus had its roots in same dynamics and logic and thus echoed that which first emerged in 1992 and re-coalesced in 1993 . Whether it also would or could be derailed through vicissitudes of personal rivalries and unforseen crises was an open question. There will of course inevitably be crises, whether caused by rivalries, economic setbacks--whether due to domestic mismanagement or foreign aid and investment manipulation or withholding--, domestic discord or external exigencies. The question is whether they will be severe enough to tip the consensus--for if tipped in the short-term its authoritarian and chauvinist pillar is likely to prevail.

*Postscript: the December 1995 Duma election and early 1996 run up to the Presidential election scheduled for June [this book went to press in April 1966] confirmed the trend. The Duma election, 'won' by the reconstituted Communist Party (with 22%, followed by Zhirinovsky's Liberal Democrats at 11%, Chernomyrdin's Our Home is Russia at 10, Yavlinsky's Yabloko at 7, and Yuri Skokov's Congress of Russian Communities--Lebed's perhaps poorly chosen affiliation--at 4%), thrust its leader, Gennady Zyuganov, into the opinion poll lead for the Presidency. Zyuganov embraced 'voluntary' re-building of the USSR, minus the Baltic states and perhaps some of Central Asia. Yeltsin fired his last 'pro-Western' Ministers, Chubais and Kosyrev (replaced by Intelligence chief Yevgeny Primakov), launched a brutal offensive to pacify Chechnya before the election, and announced the first 'coming together', a union with Belarus. Lebed, whose earlier dismissal of Ukrainian independence ('ends the day we turn off the [energy] spigot!') caught the public mood, appealed to Rutskoi and other nationalist and Communist constituencies to rally around **him**. But he lacked Zyuganov's organizational strength, and faced a Presidency desperately willing to use its powers and war chest to siphon others' votes. He had defined Russia's course, but, perhaps, lost the helm.*

Note: this chapter builds on lesser-coverage versions published in *European Security*, Winter 1993, and *War and Society*, Summer 1995. Research support from Canada's Department of Foreign Affairs and International Trade is gratefully acknowledged.

---

[268] See ie Douglas Clarke, 'Russia and the CFE Treaty', *Post-Soviet Prospects*, June 1995.

The Southern 'Near Abroad'; from Moldova to Tajikistan

6 Conclusion; How to Get There From Here

ABSTRACT: The newly urgent global threats of non-sustainable population growth, resource depletion and environmental degradation still await the necessary **doable** response that would constitute one pillar of a genuine New World Order. The spreading threat of ethno/religious exclusive nationalism and proliferating destructive potential still await the collective will and peace-keeping and -making security regime that would constitute its other pillar. Set against these criteria the New World Order proclaimed in 1991 and defined by its initial crises and crisis response patterns was a mirage. The partisan **real-politik** and old agendas that epitomized 19th. Century nation states still prevail. Yet the contradiction between New--pragmatically-required New--and Old is both unsustainable and resolvable. The parameters set for the end-of-the-Century international arena are drearily familiar to historians. Yet the agendas and solutions required for a more promising Century have also been drafted--and will ultimately have to be adopted. The changes required to ensure sustainable development prospects and sustainable global economic and security governance are addressed in this concluding chapter.

New Threats--New Agendas--New Solutions

Threats Unattended. The ever-more urgent global threats of non-sustainable population growth, resource depletion, and environmental degradation, of currencies and standards of living exposed to speculative anarchy, of largely emasculated collective decision-making and implementing will, and an increasingly skewered Old World informational menu, have all been thoroughly addressed elsewhere, as have the range of responsible, ie affordable solutions. The Brundtland Commission, Pugwash, the Worldwatch Institute, the World

110

Game Institute, UN agencies and (other) NGOs have charted what must be done and what can be done.[269]

The ever-greater urgency for change is manifest in the juxtaposition of a world of proliferating mass destruction weapons and knowledge and realities such as the following:[270]

* The absolute poor (earning less than 1 dollar a day) have increased over the last decade, from 700 million to well over 1 billion; more than 20 million die each year-- 40,000 every day--from hunger and poverty-related causes.

* Between 1960 and 1990 there was an eightfold increase in the absolute difference between the world's richest and poorest fifth--and the latter are not all in the south: one fifth of the populations in industrialized countries now also suffer from dire poverty, homelessness and malnourishment .

* Trade barriers against exportable Third World products remain higher than against those from other industrialized countries; developing countries' losses from deteriorating terms of trade alone have in many recent years exceeded the inflow of development aid.

* Developing country debt--nearing 2000 billion dollars--and repayment arrears-- well over 200 billion dollars--continue to increase, not least because the outflows of money to banks and donor governments, now over 40 billion US dollars a year, also far exceeds the total of inflowing aid. A vicious circle of immiserization indeed.

The programmes needed to address these crises have been variously costed. Worldwatch's *Reclaiming the Future* estimated the cost of programmes designed to protect topsoil and cropland, reforest, slow population growth, raise energy efficiency, develop renewable energy and retire Third World debt, each itemized and costed separately. The total cost arrived at was 124.7 billion dollars annually.

The World Game Institute costed a more ambitious agenda, with programmes designed to provide famine relief and health care for all, eliminate homelessness, ensure clean water, grant access to satellites, TV and radio, develop increased energy efficiency and sustainable energy systems, retire Third World debt and preserve natural resources, stabilize the world population, regenerate the environment, preserve cropland and reforest, stop CFC

---

[269] See The Brundtland Report, *Our Common Future*, Oxford: Oxford University Press, 1987; *Worldwatch Institute Report on Progress Towards a Sustainable Society*, New York: W.W. Norton and Co., 1988 (and successor reports); M. Gabel and E. Frisch, *Doing the Right Things*, Philadelphia: World Game Institute, 1991 (ditto); and Carl G. Jacobsen, Morris Miller, Metta Spencer And Eric Tollefson, ed.s--for Pugwash--, *World Security. The New Challenge*, Toronto: Science for Peace/Dundurn, 1994.

[270] Morris Miller, 'Global Governance to Address the Crises of Debt, Poverty and Environment', *World Security. The New Challenge*, pp 181-208.

production, end acid rain and halt global warming, also itemizing and costing each component program separately. Their total cost estimate: 255 billion dollars annually.

Some of the component program costs: a ten-year program to ensure clean and thus healthy water for all would cost 50 billion US dollars per year; a ten-year retiring of Third World debt would cost 27.3 billion dollars per year. Other cost estimates: the UN World Summit for Children costed child survival, health and education needs at 25 billion dollars; UN Peacekeeping costs jumped from 0.5 billion dollars in 1990 to 2.7 billion in 1992, and has continued to rise--a reasonable response potential in the late-90s world will probably require at least 10 billion [1995] dollars.

These are sums that can be met with no tax increase to either developed or less developed worlds.[271] The early 1990s saw world expenditures on military arms and supplies totalling over 1 trillion dollars a year. Divert just *one* percent, and you have the money needed to fund female education (the single most important development pre-requisite), family planning (where each dollar spent means a near ten dollar saving in maternal and infant care, and the saving of otherwise-expected abortion, pregnancy and birth fatalities) and improved health support programmes.[272] The ten-year programmes required for a comprehensive assault on **all** the above-described and otherwise ultimately non-containable non-military threats to human survival could be costed through re-allocation of 12-25 per cent of current military expenditures.

There are also other possible sources of 'painless' funding. The most intriguing, perhaps, is to tax the purely speculative portion of international currency transactions (these now total over a trillion dollars *a day*, of which only twenty per cent relates to trade and productive investment!). The ten-year programmes required for **sustainable development** could thus all be financed through a tax of just 0.075 per cent on just speculative currency transaction. A mere 0.003 per cent such tax would pay for all UN programmes!

One should note that funds provided, through whichever means, would have significant employment implications also for developed countries, through provision of health, welfare and other training programmes. Their advantage in science and technology would furthermore make them major beneficiaries of the development and sales potential of emergent sustainable development technologies. In Germany, which has taken the lead in this arena, 'green industry' has already become a major, rapidly expanding growth sector.

---

[271] Eric Tollefson, 'Estimating Costs and Benefits of Proposals to Create a More Secure World', *World Security. The New Challenge*, pp 249-264.

[272] Digby J. McLaren, 'Why Control Population?', *World Security. The New Challenge*, pp 127-144; see also Colette Francis' chapter in the same volume: 'Security for Future Generations: Investing in Maternal and Child Health Programs'.

Overall, it has been estimated that adoption of the World Game Institute programmes would generate between 15.5 and 16.5 million new jobs.[273]

Quintessentially, these agendas and solutions are not New World Order visions; they are defining parameters of a survivable world. The question is how to get there from here.

*

The new world's old world legacy; its lessons for the future. The proclaimed New World Order's defining crises showed a global great power community still mired in the nation state-focused **real-politik** that characterized Prince Metternich's early 19th Century Europe. Its proclivity to myth making and manipulation was no less; in fact, the wherewithal technology was now dramatically more potent--and therefore dangerous. International law also remained hostage to partisan interest, a convenience where interests coincided, a potent weapon against foes, but ignorable and ignored when inconveniently directed against self or allies.[274] The evidence points to other parameters necessary for a more meaningful and sustainable order.

*

Myth machines; the skewering of information; agenda for change. Global dominant media ownership concentration is now even more pronounced than when Noam Chomsky and Edward Hernman wrote their seminal *Manufacturing Consent.*[275] This in turn means, of course, that it is also easier to manipulate, by owner consortia and/or by PR firms and accepted advertisers. The Ruder Finn company orchestrated the appearance before Congress by the daughter of Kuwait's Washington Ambassador posing as an escaped Kuwaiti nurse, 'testifying' to utterly false horror images of babies thrown from their incubators to die--the heart rendering testimony, shown on every TV screen and every front page fuelled the march to war in the Gulf. Ruder Finn next played the lead role in the brilliant Croat PR campaign that, outspending Coca Cola and Pepsi combined, set the blame-the-Serbs moral blinkers that

---

[273] Tollefson, *op cit*, p 252.

[274] As when the Reagan administration declared The Hague International Court of Justice jurisdiction to be null and void after the Court found against Washington's not-so-covert war against Nicaragua's Sandinista government--which brought the case to the Court.

[275] Noam Chomsky and Edward S. Herman, *Manufacturing Consent*, New York: Pantheon Books, 1988; see also *Noam Chomsky and The Media*, National Film Board of Canada, 1994.

characterized Washington's and others' approach to the Yugoslav successor wars.[276] The company saw its ability to instill and embed false images as the ultimate accolade of its field; it took particular pride in the fact that *New York Times* journalists and editors so often made uncritical use of the 'information' faxed to them each morning. The *New York Times'* consequently grossly skewered decisions on what news were 'fit to print', decisions that entailed equally skewered coverage by the many who depended on its lead, was thus clearly bought by partisan money, serving partisan cause. To readers of Chomsky and history the echoing of the past was resounding.

It was also disturbing. And so was singular CNN dominance of world television news, a dominance diluted by fewer and fewer rivals; still-remaining (lesser) rivals with trans-national aspirations were in nearly every case richer-government controlled or beholden. Thus, to many, CNN came to define news and dictate their consequence. The US/UN intervened in Somalia largely because of the visceral impact of CN video clips from Mogadishu; in Sudan's even more vicious next-door civil war there were no CNN cameras, and no intervention. CNN crews reported vividly from Muslim government-held Sarajevo, but scarcely from Serb suburbs. They were not present to record early anti-Serb horrors in Croatia. Later, when ensconced also in Zagreb, they (and therefore most of the world) were likewise blind to the greater horrors of Krajina. Leading nations' G7 economic summits, NATO, the EEC and greater power problems are covered, while Non-Aligned summits and concerns, developmental and Third World problems and sorrows receive intermittent coverage at best, and often no coverage.

Chomsky points to the increasing availability of alternative news sources, such as *Z Magazine*. But even when supplemented by *Internet* anarchy and developing world media (also often government controlled) their reach is limited. The clamour for alternative news access and dissemination used to be primarily a Third World, and therefore ignorable demand. It is now increasingly a UN and industrialized world requirement; the increased dangers of faulty or incomplete intelligence are increasingly manifest.

There are obvious solutions. The UN might provide and adjudicate satellite access to developmental world news media, NGOs and alternative media channels and reporting. Democratizing formulas are feasible. Regarding military, civil and other conflicts, one might envisage equal-time guarantees, not unlike those that govern election campaigns in some developed countries. Democratized, non-money dependent and less partisan news access promises improved policy option menus for all, and lessens the dangers of excessive partisanship, deceived or deceitful decision-making and unnecessary or less worthy (ie

---

[276] As noted in chapter 4, this assumes equal rates paid for equal time.

surely most) wars. Again, a miniscule tax, say 0.001 per cent, on international speculative transactions would likely cover the necessary costs.

*

'International law'; partisan or generic? International law was clearly used for partisan political purpose through the early years of the supposed New Order, as it had been through earlier decades, and indeed earlier centuries. The Gulf War saw military action against an occupation declared illegal by Security Council majority, though none had been taken against other earlier and contemporary occupations condemned by the same body--most of which had less historical justification and less 'legal' or quasi-legal justification. Had the action been taken in the context of a universal stricture against occupations of others' land, then it might have been seen as the beginning of generic international law, law at least theoretically applying equally (even if limited means might in certain contexts and circumstance preclude immediate or effective prosecution), and not just at great power whim.

Circumvention of 'international law' for political purpose was equally evident in the New State recognitions that formalized the collapse of former Yugoslavia and the USSR. The then extension of the 'inviolate border' precept to what had been domestic administrative borders had no precedent. The only prior international agreement concerning European boundaries was that reached as part of the Helsinki Process, which sanctified those of existing states, ie federal Yugoslav and Soviet borders. The Cold War inspired haste to recognize the often dubiously democratic and sometimes outright autocratic 'democratic' governments of successor states took scant if any note of the fact that the borders these now claimed had been drawn by dictators for purposes that often had little to do with ideals of nation state demarcation.

Croatia's borders, drawn first by Nazi Germany and then Broz Tito, were deliberately drawn to incorporate ancestral Serb lands; both saw Serb nationalism as the greatest threat to their rule, and divided Serb lands as a means to minimizing the potency of the threat. Stalin gave ancestrally Armenian Nakichevan and Nagorno-Karabakh to Azerbaijan after having accepted them as part of Armenia, for he saw Armenia as having no choice other than Soviet fidelity, for memories and fears of genocide at Turkish hands precluded any other option, while Azeri loyalty was a matter to be bought. Other lands were, as we have seen, handed equally cavalierly to Lithuania, Ukraine and others. Abkhazia was handed to Georgia largely because Stalin himself was an ethnic Georgian. The uncritical extension of immunity to these contrived borders meant *ipso facto* that the secession rights now given their dominant ethnic group could not be extended to other ethnic groups on the same territory, many of whom now saw themselves as captive peoples. The refusal to give the same secession rights to ethnic groups dominant within sub-regions of the newly-independent states as had been granted those of their now dominant nationalities was in many cases indeed often prescription for war rather than peace.

The malleability of 'international law' was dramatically demonstrated a few years later when those (including Canada) who had denied Krajina and Slavonian Serbs the same secession rights from Croatia as had been granted Croats from Yugoslavia, rallied around Ottawa's contention that if the French of Quebec were to be given the right to secede from Canada, then the Cree of northern Quebec and others must be granted the equivalent right to secede from Quebec if they so wished and demonstrated through referenda. The new 'Quebec precedent' was clear reversal to the *status quo ante* of 'international law'; since its own bloody fight to quell secession the United States had always supported central government actions against secessionist rebels, even when these governments were less than reputable--until the Croatian case. Quebec's separatists took the same position as Croatia's, that 'their' borders were inviolate, no matter that (in Quebec's case also) they had been extended by federal prerogative to incorporate others' lands. But, clearly, the lack of international sanction would be a major consideration in a 'Quebec libre', as it surely also would have been to a Croatia in search of international recognition.

International law as Great Power policy tool was again evident in the 'War Crimes Tribunal' launched during the Yugoslav wars. Typified by US/UN-sanctioned accusatory forms designed for anonymous complaint and requiring no supporting evidence or testimony, and championed by US UN Ambassador Madeleine Albright--whose vigorous anti-Serb Administration-moving advocacy earned her plaudits at Ruder Finn--, this was scarcely more than a Kangaroo Court.[277] The fact that the Tribunal's investigators evinced no interest in visiting the archives of the Independent Committee on War Crimes in the Balkans in Ottawa, which collected available follow-up evidence for **all** allegations from **all** sides (and was visited by British Foreign Office, UN Peace-keeper and other international officials), or those of other non-partisan evidence collectors, was telling, and damning.

*

---

[277] This was in effect acknowledged by Canada's Colonel Fenrik, the UN point-man in terms of 'evidence collection', in a 1994 talk to the University of Ottawa's law faculty (see *ICWCB archives*, Ottawa): he acknowledged that he had neither the mandate nor resources to pursue Serb allegations and evidence, or to exhume the many graves of alleged Serb victims.

Security Borders; Security Governance: the Need For a New Prescription. You cannot propagate democracy while condemning 'captive peoples'. There are all-too-many borders that were delineated by dictators and authoritarian regimes, imposed by war or *fiat*, and sometimes specifically designed to contain ethnic mixes that would preclude viable independence; to 'recognize' these is prescription for war, not peace.

You cannot embrace the 'right to independence' of secessionist minded 'democratically elected' governments and then stand back when [for example] Georgia's Gamsakhurdia declares minorities with roots that go back more than a millennium to have arrived too recently to deserve full citizenship.

You cannot accept the denial of civil rights to Baltic Russian populations because many settled there after Stalin's murderous pogroms against nationalists and Nazi collaborators. Many had ancestors who lived in these lands before World War 1, who had been killed or exiled by German arms in 1917, and by British-supplied bayonets in the civil war that followed.

The point is not to disparage the yearnings of Croats, Lithuanians, Azeris or others. Nor is it to note that some of these lands are like Palestine, where all can find earlier injustices to justify theirs. The note is important. In Bosnia cultural prejudices are steeped in 'memories' of more than a thousand years of slight and counter-slight, massacres and counter-massacres; when the past is unleashed, innocence falls victim. So also elsewhere.

The point is that there are some contexts where elementary notions of democracy demand either reciprocal border adjustments to produce more homogeneous populations, **or** truly effective, Swiss **Canton**-like and/or other guarantees for minorities.[278] The former is particularly problematic in places such as Croatia and some Soviet successor states. The Austro-Hungarian and Russian empires were different in kind, leaving a legacy of ethnic mix that defy easy 'withdrawal'; the roots are too deep, the numbers too large.

In older world orders the security of the state took precedence. If the New World Order is to be different, then precedence must shift to the **security**--including rights and equal opportunity--of groups and individuals, minorities of mind and circumstance. Democracy as majority rule does not suffice; democracy must be minority protective. Rights must be inclusive, not exclusive, and universal, not parochial.

At the other end of the scale it must also transcend the traditional bounds and prerogatives of the nation state. This demands a transcendant authority, a genuinely revitalized, more potent and more representative United Nations. This in turn demands expansion of the Security Council's permanent membership to Germany, Japan, India and

---

[278] Metta Spencer, 'How to Enhance Democracy and Discourage Secession', *World Security. The New Challenge*, pp 161-178.

perhaps Indonesia, Nigeria and/or South Africa, Brazil, and possibly Argentina, so as to end the exclusion of non-nuclear states and continents. It also demands dilution of the veto power. Single-power veto in an expanded Council would be crippling. Yet existing veto powers would surely veto the 'democratic' alternative of no veto. Might they have the confidence to accept a diluted half or one-third veto right--whereby the concurring votes of one or two others would be needed to thwart the majority will?

More effective peace-keeping and -making would also require stand-by military potential, staff and logistics far beyond that presently envisaged. It demands a qualifying and limiting of sovereignty for which few are ready, least of all the Great Powers. And there would always be the danger that the cure proved worse than the decease. The prospect of an omnipotent UN **bureautocracy** is not altogether reassuring. It is also *the* reason why a more potent UN *must* be a more democratic UN.

Whatever the compromises that evolve, whether at the lowest or highest level, suffice to say that when nation state histories incorporate more of those of other nation states **as well as** those of their own and others' minorities, then we shall have a different world--not a New World Order, for that may be as dangerous as it is naive (Hitler also spoke of a New World Order), but a more civilized, and tolerant world. Maybe the achieving is in the striving.

Index

120

Note on Author:

Professor Carl G. Jacobsen is **Director** of the **Eurasian Security Studies** Organized Research Unit [ORU], Political Science Department, **Carleton University**, and Consultant on post-Soviet, Eurasian and security issues. He received his Ph.D. (on Strategic Factors in Soviet foreign policy) from Glasgow University in 1971. He has taught at Glasgow University; Miami, Columbia and Harvard Universities in the United States; and Carleton, Acadia and McGill Universities in Canada. He has served as Director of Soviet and Strategic Studies at the University of Miami's Graduate School of International Studies (1980-85), as Director of Soviet Studies and Senior Research Officer at the Stockholm International Peace Research Institute (1985-87), and as Director of Carleton's Institute of Soviet and East European Studies (1990-1992). Professor Jacobsen is the author of five books, editor and co-author of another six, and has written more than 100 refereed and/or commissioned articles. His latest books are *The Soviet Defence Enigma: Estimating Costs and Burden* and *The Uncertain Course: New Arms, Strategies and Mindsets* (Oxford University Press, 1987); *Soviet Foreign Policy; new dynamics, new themes* and *Strategic Power: USA/USSR* (Macmillan and St. Martin's Press, 1989 and 1990), and *World Security; The New Challenge* (Pugwash--Science for Peace / Dundurn, 1994).

124